The Serving Leader

For the People of God

5 Powerful Actions That Will Transform Your Team Your Church and Your Community

ELIZABETH WOURMS & JOHN STAHL-WERT

Table of Contents

Introduction

*The God of Israel spoke, the Rock of Israel said to me:
"When one rules over men in righteousness, when he rules
in the fear of God, he is like the light of morning at sunrise
on a cloudless morning, like the brightness after rain that
brings the grass from the earth."*
(2 Samuel 23:3-4)[1]

There are many books on leadership. There are many books on Christian leadership. Our hope is that you have selected this book because you want to lead people in a way that glorifies God—modeling the serving leadership of Jesus, and shining "like the light of morning at sunrise on a cloudless morning" in encouraging many.

The Purpose of This Book
This book is designed for Christian leaders serving in churches, faith-based organizations and Christian schools and universities. Its purpose is to:

---

1   Unless otherwise indicated, all Scripture references are from the New International Version.

* Engage leaders in biblical and theological reflection
* Guide the reader toward applying serving leadership principles in practical and relevant ways
* Be a catalyst for personal and community transformation in the lives of people

Whether you are a leader in a congregation, a non-profit organization, parachurch ministry, a seminary or university—this book will equip and encourage you to further embody Serving Leadership in your life and ministry. The content is geared toward anyone actively involved in church and faith-based work—volunteers, ordained persons, paid and non-paid staff members, educators, consultants, trainers.

This book is based upon Stahl-Wert and Jennings' *The Serving Leader* text. If you have not read it, we encourage you to lay this book aside for the moment and engage *The Serving Leader: 5 Powerful Actions That Will Transform Your Team, Your Business and Your Community* (Berrett-Koehler Publishers, 2003, 2004). You will find in the Prologue of *The Serving Leader For the People of God* a basic overview of *The Serving Leader*.

Distinctives of the Christian Serving Leader

As Christians, we exist to glorify God by living totally for Him out of love for Him. In what we call "The Greatest Commandment," Jesus summarizes God's desire for us: "'Love the Lord your God with all your heart and with all your soul and with all your mind.' This is the first and greatest commandment. And the second is like it: 'Love your neighbor as yourself.' All

2

the Law and the Prophets hang on these two commandments" (Matthew 22:37-40).

Serving God is a primary way of loving Him. Serving God by serving people is then one avenue we have for responding to God's great love for us. One of the ways we serve people best is by leading them—leading them to grow in relationship with Jesus Christ, and leading them in such a way that they flourish and become all God wants them to be. We believe **Serving Leadership** is the way God would have us lead others. As we will see in this book, God has a lot to say about serving leadership, and Jesus perfectly demonstrated what this looks like in action.

As Serving Leaders, God has given Christians many wonderful distinctive resources:

* Continuous access to Him and His wisdom through prayer
* A model to follow—Jesus
* Power to lead—the Holy Spirit
* An instruction book—the Bible
* Leadership gifts
* Forgiveness from God for when we blow it!

These distinctives are for Serving Leaders who have given themselves to Jesus Christ as Savior and Lord. When we speak of Serving Leaders in this particular book, we do so with this unique understanding.

Format of the Book

The five actions of a Serving Leader brought forth in The Serving Leader form the principle areas of focus in this book. In this text, the five actions are specifically applied to Christian leadership inside and alongside the church. Each chapter examines one of the "5 Powerful Actions" in theory and practice.

You will see that each chapter begins with a foundational Scripture, a definition of the Serving Leader action, and its paradox. This is followed by a brief fictional narrative that introduces the topic. After a chapter overview, we then provide biblical/theological sections, followed by suggestions for practical application. A real-life story is then given to illustrate how the Serving Leader action has worked in an actual church or Christian organization setting. Each chapter concludes with a closing thought and a few questions for reflection.

Ultimately, our desire is that this book be intensely **practical**. In other words, **we want this material to truly make a difference in how and why you lead the people that God has placed around you.** After all, if this text is not a useful resource for your personal growth and development—indeed a catalyst for lasting change and transformation—then it is really of no use at all. Toward that end, we have included questions for reflection throughout each of the chapters. You will find space provided to record your thoughts, questions, discoveries, and action steps.

As you read this book, you will also notice a small headphones symbol at various places throughout. In an effort to better appeal to the variety of learning styles and preferences among adult learners, the authors recorded a series of podcasts to accompany the text. The headphone symbol indicates that a podcast related to that particular topic is available at www.johnstahlwert.com/TSL. These audio conversations invite you into further reflection and engagement on particular topics being addressed. If you discover that you would benefit from additional training, coaching, or mentoring around key competencies lifted up in the text, we would welcome a conversation with you about opportunities that exist. Please feel free to communicate with us through the contact information at the back of this book.

Finally, Serving Leaders demonstrate unified lives. They recognize that all of life is ministry and all of ministry is life. Serving Leaders authentically and transparently embody the attitudes, postures, and practices of Serving Leadership at home, in their neighborhoods, in their places of worship, in their work, at play, in all their pursuits and interests. **Serving Leadership is a way of life.**

Serving Leadership is inherently paradoxical. This lifestyle turns conventional wisdom and practice on its head. In the pages that follow, we invite you into this life-giving journey of discovery and paradox. May the Lord bless you and transform you into a true Serving Leader as you read, reflect, and put into practice what you learn.

Prologue

"We should not feel embarrassed by our difficulties, only by our failure to grow anything beautiful from them."
Alain De Botton

The essential beginning to this book—the road less traveled; the journey toward promise.

Sometimes a concept or ideal is best described by what it is not, rather than what it is. By traveling the via negativa, the seeker experiences the shadow side of the thing, peeking into the corners and daring to step down dark alleys in order to discover what must not be in order to enter into the better way. This book is about the better way—the pathway of Serving Leadership, a life-giving journey for both the one serving and those being served. It is an ideal to be pursued as we follow hard after the footsteps of our Lord Jesus Christ. But this book dare not take a sanguine path, a road paved with good intentions and happy endings—such a highway serves no one well and only positions the reader to be blindsided by the obstacles and barriers lurking around the next curve. We'll get

to that joyous place, that better way because our God is the
God of the leveled plain, of rough places made smooth, of
raised valleys (Isaiah 40:3-5). The journey begins, however,
on a broken road, on the very rough places that we often seek
to avoid, in the wilderness that we fear. Just as winter is a pre-
lude to spring, in exile we sing songs of lament and yet hear
the voice of promise calling out the response.

What is this via negativa, this darker path? Far from being the
opposite (which might be hastily characterized as selfish ambition, vain conceit, narcissism, or apathy and complacency) of
Serving Leadership, the shadow of this ideal bears witness to a
darker, more insidious reality. **Simply put, Serving pushed to
an extreme becomes destructive**—caustic to the servant and
unhelpful to those being served. Super-Serving-Leadership
is a ravenous beast that stalks and then moves in for the kill
when its prey is least suspecting. This predator is no figment
of a delusional imagination. It is a living reality and it waits
for you, dear reader. That is why this book must begin in the
wilderness, in the place where this monster lurks. Only after
we expose it and its cunning ways, can we turn to the ideal and
journey down the roadway toward Serving Leadership. Rest
assured our goal in writing is to picture the ideal and invite
you to enter into it, to cultivate aspiration within you, to catalyze transformation in your life and ministry. Perhaps a greater goal becomes to save you from yourself so that you might be
freed to embark on this better way.

Sculpting the ideal is risky business anyway. As the figure takes
shape, the reader may despair, I can never look like that; pre-

sented with flawless lines and blemish-less form, the reader may lament, I've never even known anyone who approximates an incarnation of that ideal. Like a super-model, this sculpted beauty remains elusive, out of reach of the majority. In this book we endeavor to paint a realistic picture of Serving Leadership—one that is not only within reach, but actually embraceable.

The Ministry Wilderness

The city limits sign at the outskirts of the ministry wilderness reads, Busyness and Over-functioning, pop. 1. When entering the ministry, we didn't set out to populate this territory; that was not our goal, nor did we have any conscious awareness that this terrain existed. Sensing a call from God into full-time, vocational ministry, we charted our course with all the zeal of a new postulant. Here am I, Lord; send me! (Isaiah 6:8) became our fervent cry. Desire to serve, to minister, to lead, to shepherd fueled our pursuit of the call.

It is a worthy desire, this desire to serve. It is God-breathed. Serving stands as a noble embodiment of a biblical ideal—indeed Christ Himself is Serving Incarnate. So what could possibly be wrong with living a life of service under the call of God? On the surface, nothing is wrong with it. The shadow side lurks, however, and the savvy leader risks peering into the shadows in order to discover how to more fully abide in the light. **The first footstep into the shadows, into the wilderness, is revealed in the sand around one's motivations for serving.**

My motivations are pure, you may counter. I serve because I'm called by God and desire to help people. The skeptic lobbies back at you, nobody's motives are that pure; a hidden agenda always exists. The prophet Isaiah offers the truth, "All of us have become like one who is unclean, and all our righteous acts are like filthy rags…" (Isaiah 64:6). Isaiah cautions us that even our best efforts, our noblest attempts, our purest service are tainted by sin and hence forever marred. Indeed God redeems and transforms our offerings and uses them for Kingdom purposes; but in our own human strength, we possess no righteousness nor can we offer righteousness in service to others. A slippery slope into a "good deeds" marsh awaits those who navigate this path of service. The service itself dilutes reliance upon God's grace and the guidance of the Holy Spirit until the servant winds up swimming by her own strength—a "Martha" if you will—treading in the waters of ministry.

Sometimes God calls us toward greater self-awareness by inviting us to plumb the depths of our consciousness to explore hidden motivations. The Apostle Paul would not have divulged the following were he not struggling with ulterior motives: "Am I now trying to win the approval of men, or of God? Or am I trying to please men? If I were still trying to please men, I would not be a servant of Christ" (Galatians 1:10). **For many ministers of the Gospel, clergy and laity, much service is cloaked in our need for approval; our need to be appreciated; our need to be recognized; our need to be affirmed.** A willingness to enter into conversation with our own motivators exposes driving forces and challenges assumptions and preconceptions. Begin this conversation with yourself gently and be sure to offer yourself grace as this inner dialogue may be painful and difficult. Suffice it to say, we each have impediments to healthy, authentic Serving Leadership.

A Personal Word about the "Ministry Wilderness" from Elizabeth Wourms

My own spiritual obstacle is busyness and over-functioning. Perhaps you can relate. If not, I invite you to look into my journey through the window of your own challenges and issues and then look into the mirror to process what you see.

Busyness became for me not only the destination but the vehicle that transported me there. Busyness was my personal Babylon; over-functioning arrived as my Babylonian defeater. This cunning captor dragged me into exile along a primrose path. For many years, I didn't realize I was enslaved; I certainly had no awareness of how I'd gotten there.

Somewhere along the way, grace was ambushed, and ministry—serving—became about doing. In my zeal to be obedient to God's call, in my fervor to live for Christ and to be sold out to the Gospel, I busied myself with godly tasks. I've always been a competent doer and ambitious striver, so pouring myself whole-heartedly into ministry pursuits came naturally. It was easy to become ambitious for God. As a person with many interests and a diverse portfolio of gifts and skills, I find it easy to become immersed in a multitude of activities all at once. The Babylonian captor whispered in my ear and deceived me into believing that "living for the Lord" meant being "on the clock" for ministry 24/7.

Once upon a time, I'd dedicated my life to the Lord Jesus Christ and embarked on a life of service in His Name and for His Kingdom. Somewhere along the way I gave my life over to the Church and to the work of the ministry. This false "giving over" opened the door for the Babylonians to enter. Thus began the journey into exile.

When God called Moses into ministry and dispatched him for service, God revealed Himself as I AM. This sending God, the One who creates and calls, reveals the Divine Self in terms of being. Out of the glorious mystery that is the Holy Trinity, flows the startling declaration that God will not be defined according to function and action, but rather by the essence of identity. "God said to Moses, 'I AM WHO I AM. This is what you are to say to the Israelites: I AM has sent me to you.' God also said to Moses, 'Say to the Israelites, The LORD, the God of your fathers—the God of Abraham, the God of Isaac and the God of Jacob—has sent me to you. This is my name forever, the name by which I am to be remembered from generation to generation'" (Exodus 3:14-15). Out of God's being, God sends. **As beings created in God's image, it is out of our being—out of our identity that we go.** God invites us to serve and to minister secure in our identity as beloved children, surrounded by Christ's love and grace, fueled by His Holy Spirit. God urges us to live and move and have our being in Him (Acts 17:28); not to live and strive and behave as "human doings." The Apostle Paul grasped this truth and declared, "In him [Christ] we were also chosen... in order that we, who were the first to hope in Christ, might be for the praise of his glory" (Ephesians 1:11-12). Why is it that as God's chosen, as God's beloved, that we choose to do and strive and labor, rather than simply to be?

Paul goes on elsewhere to characterize the life of God's chosen ones. "Therefore, as God's chosen people, holy and dearly loved, clothe yourselves with compassion, kindness, humility, gentleness and patience... And over all these virtues put on love..." (Colossians 3:12-14). Secure in our identity as God's beloved, we are to clothe ourselves with life-giving attributes. **When we are not secure in our identity as God's beloved, we clothe ourselves with costumes.** Just as Adam and Eve donned fig leaves to cover their shame and nakedness, when we don't like what we see as we look into our inner mirror, we browse our "closets" for what we deem to be suitable coverings. I adopted busyness as my personal mantle.

Arriving at a place of profound burnout and exhaustion in my Babylon, I entered into a season of deep discernment and reflection. In this wilderness experience, in this dark night of the soul, I cried out to God, confused and disillusioned and uncertain of the way out—the way toward promise. By the rivers of Babylon I sat and wept as I remembered my Zion—the call of God into Kingdom-building and I sang songs of lament over lost and broken dreams and relationships and the call polluted by my own dysfunction (Psalm 137: 1). Exile taught me many things, and God revealed to me that I had covered myself in busyness as a means to seek approval and find fulfillment.

I awakened to the fact that my sense of self had become wrapped up in excelling and accomplishing. Achievement fueled my self-esteem; recognition and position drove me. Remember, God issued a call to full-time vocational ministry, and I labored out of love for God and zeal to see Christ's Kingdom come and His will be done. This was a noble and God-ordained pursuit. My hidden need to accomplish, however, joined forces with my zeal for ministry, and the result was that **serving became the god I worshipped.** In the wilderness, I fell exhausted and spent under the heavy yoke I had chosen to wear, never having come to understand how Christ's yoke can be easy and His burden light (Matthew 11:28-30). I fought hard to protect my self-image with the "good" things that sub-consciously defined me because I equated these things with God's love and approval. I realized that I had never fully owned my identity in Christ, never completely surrendered myself to God's grace, never allowed myself to bask in the glow of God's love and simply to be.

Serving In Vain

When well-intentioned servants labor out of any identity other than the one bestowed by the Great I AM—the Eternal Being who creates in His image, they labor in vain. False identities lead human beings to become human doings, robots veiled in sheep's clothing, moving mechanistically under the influence of their own power. Human doings may perform good deeds; indeed noble service and helpful initiatives may thrive and flourish. Churches and non-profit organizations may "thrive and flourish" according to outward appearance, but a better way exists.

God calls us not to "good deeds"—lives characterized by works righteousness, by pharisaical pursuit of favor and accomplishment. God loves us too much to allow us to settle for that. Christ died to redeem us from that. God's love compels us first to be, to exist for the praise of His glory, to abide in His presence, to be fueled by the Holy Spirit, to enter into Christ's shalom. Secondly, God's love invites us to respond gracefully out of that place of abundance, in accordance with the movement of the Spirit in the rhythm of God's Kingdom enterprises. Finally, as we come to greater self-awareness about who God has uniquely created and called us to be, we become better able to find our niche for ministry—a specific and focused avenue for service. Serving Leaders know what is theirs to do and are able to say "Yes!" to initiatives that match their gifts and skill sets and lend themselves to truly life-giving opportunities. Serving Leaders courageously say "No!" to life-depleting initiatives that might match certain skill sets but lie outside the boundaries of God's specific invitation to find that place in which to spread wings and fly.

Paul discovered this key to life and life in abundance. He describes his efforts for the Gospel, "To this end I labor, struggling with all his [Christ's] energy, which so powerfully works in me" (Colossians 1:29), and "I have learned the secret of being content in any and every situation... I can do everything through him [Christ] who gives me strength" (Philippians 4:11-13). Paul labored, not in his own strength but through Christ's. Paul experienced shalom because he learned in the dark night of his own soul that it was only through Christ that he could accomplish anything. Out of our being flows Christ's doing.

This formula: [being + Christ's doing] forms the starting point for Serving Leadership. Once those ingredients come together, a powerful reaction ignites infinite possibilities and the power of Serving Leadership is unleashed.

A Personal Word about The Serving Leader from John Stahl-Wert

The Serving Leader, co-authored with my friend, Ken Jennings, was first published in 2003. Quickly, the book became a bestselling favorite for students of servant leadership, and a beloved story of personal, organizational, and community transformation for men and women around the world. Translated into eight languages, including Chinese, Korean, Indonesian, German, Portuguese and others, The Serving Leader has grown, year by year, in sales and reach.

Ken and I attribute the book's success to the biblical principles upon which the book is founded. We are both followers of Jesus, and from the beginning built upon a biblical framework in the writing of our book. Simply stated, the leadership principles that work best in the world are the leadership teachings of Jesus; true success in leadership can be founded upon nothing else.

The Serving Leader outlines "Five Powerful Actions" that serving leaders must learn and practice. These "Actions" are very practical in nature, as opposed to theoretical. A regular human being can understand each "Action," can learn how to practice each "Action," and can teach others. In the same way that "professional Christians" aren't needed to advance God's mighty purposes in the world, "professional leaders" aren't needed to achieve extraordinary results in the world. Regular human beings, yielded to God's will and design, are the leaders who actually make the greatest positive difference through their leadership for the world.

The "Five Actions" of the Serving Leader are:

1. *Run to Great Purpose*—serving leaders must provide their followers and their organizations with a truly compelling vision—a reason why—for their lives and work. The book and its training resources teach leaders how to do this.
2. *Upend the Pyramid*—serving leaders must put themselves at the bottom of their organization in order to serve the success and accomplishment of the people who work for them. The book shows leaders how to make this shift in position and attitude.
3. *Raise the Bar*—serving leaders must establish an organizational culture of excellence and high engagement by leading from values. The book and its training resources coach leaders how to grow in discipline and integrity in the course of daily management.
4. *Blaze the Trail*—serving leaders must teach the business distinctives of their enterprise and remove the distractions and obstacles that hinder their team members as well as progress. The book shows leaders how to make mission clear, and keep great focus on those essentials that are at the heart of success.
5. *Build on Strength*—serving leaders must know what the capabilities and passions of their workers are in order

to build strengths-based and complementary teams.
The book and its training resources guide leaders to
know their workers strengths and to build strong team
alignments.

Run to Great Purpose

For Christ's love compels us, because we are convinced that one died for all, and therefore all died. And he died for all, that those who live should no longer live for themselves but for him who died for them and was raised again.

(2 Corinthians 5:14-15)

Definition: Serving leaders Run to Great Purpose by holding out in front of their team, business, or community a 'reason why' that is so big that it requires and motivates everybody's very best effort.

Paradoxes: To do the most possible good, strive for the impossible. Sustain the self's greatest interest in pursuits beyond self-interest.

 Narrative

Pastor John was the last to leave the church. After locking the door to the parking lot, he looked up at the evening sky and saw the summer stars silently glimmering. The board meeting had gone much longer than he had anticipated. Much longer. With a long sigh he eased into his car and headed for home.

"OK, Lord... What was that all about?" he muttered half sarcastically. He hoped his wife was not waiting up for him.

She was. "John, you're much later than you said you would be. Don't you think you give enough hours to the church? What was it this time?"

John, slumping down in a kitchen chair, could tell a short answer wasn't going to cut it for Mary, but he started out slowly. "Well, the board started talking about the future direction of the church..."

He paused, staring off into space.

His wife had seen this look before. She softened and touched his hand. "John, tell me what happened..."

John refocused and said, "Mary, all I know is that all of a sudden the discussion we were having about purchasing a stupid riding lawnmower for church maintenance turned into a free-for-all about the budget and where the church is going."

He closed his eyes, rewinding the draining drama that had just played out. "It was as if a dam broke and each person had to talk louder and more forcefully than the person before... 'More Sunday School classes! Better community presence! Focus on young families with children! More contemporary worship! More traditional worship!... and Pastor, why aren't you visiting in the hospital more?'... And Mary, get this one—one person, you can imagine who, was adamant about cutting staff salaries, saying 'I don't see why the pastor and staff need to make more than I do...'"

"Mary," he said, looking back into space, and then back into her tearing eyes, "I don't know any more... I just don't know. I thought the Lord called me into ministry, but I just don't know any more... All the fun is gone."

📚 Chapter Overview

The thesis for this chapter is simple: A strong sense of **personal purpose** paves the way for a robust sense of **team or organizational purpose.** Leaders who understand their own "reason why"—the peculiar passion that burns in their bones, the compelling vision that catapults them into daily action—are better able to accomplish three things: align themselves with a team or organization that shares the same burning passion; occupy a focused niche within that entity that matches well with personal giftedness and skill sets; and champion the entity's vision such that it motivates everyone's best effort. Leaders who flounder are often lacking one or more of those three key ingredients for success and effectiveness, or possess only a vague understanding of personal and/or organizational purpose.

Serving Leaders Run to Great Purpose while simultaneously holding two banners out in front:

* *Personal purpose and stated mission*—compelling reason why that guides personal disciplines and vocational choices and motivates personal best effort

* *Team and organizational purpose and stated mission*—compelling reason why that motivates everyone's best effort

 **Biblical Foundations**

Personal Purpose

Our purpose as human beings is to glorify God. We live this worshipful life purposefully as we discover a unique sense of personal purpose, or life mission. Purposeful living embodies God's invitation to "offer your bodies as living sacrifices, holy and pleasing to God—this is your spiritual act of worship" (Romans 12: 1b). Scripture offers many examples of people who demonstrated a clear understanding of their life mission. Following are a few snapshots.

John the Baptist

When questioned about his identity and purpose, John answered, "I am the voice of one calling in the desert, 'Make straight the way for the Lord'" (John 1:23b). John further clarified, "the reason I came baptizing with water was that he [Jesus] might be revealed to Israel... the one who sent me to baptize with water told me, 'The man on whom you see the Spirit come down and remain is he who will baptize with the Holy Spirit'" (John 1:31b, 33b). John pursued his "call to ministry" zealously and with great conviction. Within the broad call, John recognized that his specific mission was to herald Jesus' arrival and to baptize people.

Jesus

Jesus himself possessed a clear understanding of his own life mission. He said, "I have come that they may have life, and have it to the full" (John 10:10). Elsewhere he declared, "For the Son of Man came to seek and to save what was lost" (Luke 19:10); "For even the Son of Man did not come to be served, but to serve, and to give his life as a ransom for many" (Mark 10:45). Each of the Scriptures cited lends depth and nuance to Jesus' mission. His clearly defined mission guided every attitude and activity of his life. Yours can, too.

Jeremiah

The Prophet Jeremiah exemplifies another biblical leader who heard clearly and responded to his unique and specific life mission. God declared, "Before I formed you in the womb I knew you, before you were born I set you apart; I appointed you as a prophet to the nations." (Jeremiah 1:5). God invites you to appropriate that good word for yourself. Imagine God whispering to you, "Before I formed you in the womb I knew you, before you were born I set you apart; I appointed you as a _____." What do you hear the voice of God saying to you about God's plans and purposes for your life?

Paul

The Apostle Paul frequently found himself in the position of needing to defend his life mission. Paul asserted, "And for this purpose I was appointed a herald and an apostle—I am telling the truth, I am not lying—and a teacher of the true faith to the Gentiles (1 Timothy 2:7); Paul, an apostle—sent not from men nor by man, but by Jesus Christ and God the Father, who raised him from the dead… they saw that I had been entrusted with the task of preaching the gospel to the Gentiles…" (Galatians 1:1; 2:7). Paul clearly understood that his life mission was to be an apostle to the Gentiles, a champion of the Good News to a specific people-group. His call was not to preach to the Jews or to disciple emerging rabbis or to minister to widows and orphans—important as those functions were. God called Paul to proclaim the Gospel to a particular people. Period.

As a Serving Leader pursuing your call to ministry, are you able to proclaim like Paul, "For this purpose I was appointed a _____, entrusted with the task of ____ _____"? Reflect.

Leadership Challenges

Many leaders jump into the vast sea that is the "call to ministry," and begin swimming feverishly only to become exhausted and overwhelmed by the vastness and enormity of it. Tragically, a majority of these leaders drown, never knowing that a safe harbor existed for them just around a bend; a place appointed specifically for them, a place where a unique and God-ordained function awaited them. For example, you may pursue a call to pastor a church, or serve as a missionary, or function as a Christian educator. Those positions usually entail a vast array of roles and tasks; frequently people are asked to shoulder an enormous burden of responsibility within a single position. As pastor, you may be expected to preach, teach, perform Sacraments, visit the sick and shut-in, lead meetings, cast vision, manage administrative functions, oversee finances, supervise staff, maintain the physical plant, plan worship services… the list is unending. The challenge most days becomes effectively juggling many balls, and success is measured by the number of balls in the air.

Imagine the pastoral (or any ministry) role (in all its many facets) as a large, colorful puzzle with each piece representing a particular function. Which piece(s) of the puzzle has God uniquely prepared for you? In what **focused niche** would you best fit? One way to identify your piece of the ministry puzzle is to respond to statements such as, "I feel most alive when I perform these tasks: _____." "These sorts of functions are life-giving, or energizing for me: _____ _____." "These sorts of tasks drain me of energy: _____." "My gift-mix, abilities, skill-sets, and passion make me best suited for the following roles and tasks: _____ _____."

Serving Leaders "peel back the layers" of the "ministry onion" in order to discover **the core of their calling**, that aspect of God's Kingdom work that they simply cannot leave undone. Serving Leaders identify, equip, and release others to live their calling by helping them fulfill necessary functions and tasks alongside the Serving Leader. If your unique passion is teaching and preaching, then empower those people whose passion is visitation, administration, etc. to become part of your team. Everyone will be motivated to give their best effort and the team will Run to Great Purpose **together**.

As Serving Leaders embody personal purpose, they invite

others in the organization into a similar journey of discovery through their example and encouragement. As increasing numbers of people within the organization tap into their personal purpose, energy and excitement swells around living robustly into the organization's purpose and mission. Leaders become better able to live and work within their own "sweet spot" for ministry and to authentically delegate roles and responsibilities to gifted others. Personal and team morale increases; exhaustion and burnout decreases. Later in this chapter, we will explore further methods by which to assess mission and purpose; the chapter Build on Strength offers insights on the ways in which God gifts and calls people for ministry.

Serving Leaders

Serving Leaders who run to great purpose don't run aimlessly. They run purposefully. Through the Word, God invites leaders to emulate the example of people like John, Paul, Jeremiah, and our Lord Jesus Christ by prayerfully articulating a clear, concise, and compelling sense of personal mission. The Apostle Paul declared, "For [you] are God's workmanship, created in Christ Jesus to do good works, which God prepared in advance for [you] to do" (Ephesians 2:10). No greater affirmation coupled with evocative invitation exists in all of Scripture. **You** are God's workmanship. **You** are a wondrous product of God's infinitely creative imagination. Such a realization should both humble and exhilarate you.

God created you, not to set you on a shelf and admire you, but for the purpose of good works—and not just any good works but ones for God's Kingdom enterprises—for those specific pieces of the Kingdom-puzzle that are custom-designed for you. The Message translation renders Ephesians 2:10, "[God] creates each of us by Christ Jesus to join him in the work he does, the good work he has gotten ready for us to do, work we had better be doing." A more literal translation of the last part of the phrase from the original Greek states, "... good works which God previously prepared in order that we might walk in them." As a child, you may have followed footsteps in the snow or mud, carefully making sure that your small feet lined up exactly, step by step with the footprints laid out before you. So it is when leaders carefully identify the steps they are to take—the ones marked out in advance by God—and walk in them. Serving Leaders who Run to Great Purpose don't run aimlessly. They run purposefully. Purposeful leaders catalyze the formation of purposeful teams and organizations. Serving Leaders chart a purposeful course, confident that God will direct and determine their steps (Proverbs 16:9).

I praise you because I am fearfully and wonderfully made; your works are wonderful... All the days ordained for me were written in your book before one of them came to be (Psalm 139:14, 16).

I cry out to God Most High, to God, who fulfills {his purpose} for me (Psalm 57:2).

The LORD will fulfill {his purpose} for me; your love, O LORD, endures forever—do not abandon the works of your hands (Psalm 138:8).

 (Visit www.johnstahlwert.com/TSL for podcast #1 on

"The People of God Need Serving Leaders.")

Organizational Purpose

In order to describe organizational purpose at the corporate level, it is helpful to progress toward it from the individual level:

* The purpose of humanity is to glorify God (Ephesians 1: 12; Exododus 9: 16).
* The purpose of Serving Leaders is to embody their own unique gifts/skills for ministry (1 Peter 4:10), and equip others for service, releasing the gifts of the people (Ephesians 4:12).
* The purpose of the Church is to manifest the Kingdom of God as it makes disciples (Matthew 28: 18-20).

Before a particular church can become truly effective at disciple-making (both privilege and responsibility), that local fellowship must clarify its understanding of some key concepts. Never take for granted or assume that the people in the pews understand what it means to be the Church. Or perhaps better stated: understand that each person who self-identifies with your congregation will have a different definition or connotation around what it means to be "church." **In order to clarify organizational purpose, first clarify identity**[2]. Once you gain

---

2 Undertaking a series of focus groups or other discussion-based exercises for the expressed purpose of articulating your congregation's definition of the Body of Christ—the Church—can be life-giving. Two pastoral colleagues gained that clarity with their congregations. Rev. Dr. G. Edwin Zeiders defines the Church as, "A Spirit-filled, redemptive community driving the folk into culture. The end goal is martyrdom, not membership. The church is a mission outpost." Rev. Dr. R. Robert Creech led his

clarity regarding your identity as the Body of Christ, explore what it means to "be a disciple," and then to make disciples in the context of realms such as Worship, Faith Formation (Bible study, spiritual disciplines, service, etc.), Outreach, and Forming Community. How will you develop internal systems and accountability structures in order to ensure that you live and grow faithfully in these arenas and the overall mission of disciple-making?[3]

Under the over-arching umbrella of disciple-making (the Greatest Commandment and the Great Commission of our Lord Jesus Christ) lies the unique and peculiar heartbeat of each specific congregation's mission. Just as the New Testament churches exemplified particular cultures, characteristics, qualities, and vision, so do congregations today. God invites your local fellowship to a focused piece of Kingdom-building. Which unique piece of the larger puzzle are you? **Raising up and sustaining a unique and honed vision/mission with a corresponding plan that connects success to the daily work of God's people is essential to running to great purpose.**

All this becomes the ongoing work of the leaders and congregation. You'll know that you're running to great purpose

---

congregation in a self-study and determined, "The Church is an intentional, Spirit-filled community of followers of Jesus Christ engaging the mission of God." After articulating the definitions, these leaders facilitated conversations with congregation members in order to further clarify the terms and concepts inherent in the definitions. Such a series of exercises may prove fruitful for you, as well.

3   If you are a leader in an organization other than a church, translate the principles from this section of the text into your own context. Pursue a similar exercise in clarifying organizational identity and purpose.

when your staffing plan, annual budget, team structure, congregational culture, programs and initiatives all align under the banner of a compelling stated mission/purpose. Serving Leaders commit themselves to this process with unwavering zeal, determination, and perseverance. They celebrate their purpose as human beings, embrace their purpose as leaders, and champion the purpose of the Church. Humanly, all these endeavors are impossible. Serving Leaders cling to God's mandate and promise, "seek first his kingdom and his righteousness, and all these things will be given to you as well" (Matthew 6:33). Paradoxically, in order to be a contributor in God's Kingdom enterprises, you must strive for the impossible. The impossible becomes possible through the empowerment of the Holy Spirit.

Serving Leaders within parachurch ministries or non-profit organizations explore similar questions of identity and purpose and develop the same types of systems, pathways, and processes for living into their stated vision and mission.

The Exodus narrative is one striking biblical account that paints a compelling picture of Run to Great Purpose. At the burning bush, God proclaims to Moses, "I have indeed seen the misery of my people in Egypt. I have heard them crying out because of their slave drivers, and I am concerned about their suffering. So I have come down to rescue them from the hand of the Egyptians and to bring them up out of that land into a good and spacious land, a land flowing with milk and honey... So now, go. I am sending you to Pharaoh to bring my people the Israelites out of Egypt" (Exodus 3: 7-10). With great clarity and conviction, God asserts the contributing circumstances and the ensuing vision and mission; God summons Moses to Run to Great Purpose. Israel's pursuit of that purpose involves a 40-year wilderness adventure toward the promised outcome (Exodus 3–40; Joshua 1–4).

Serving Leaders can take heart and encouragement from the biblical narrative. As you Run to Great Purpose, know that the road will be fraught with danger, disappointment, set-backs, discouragement, and heartbreak. God does not promise an easy journey. God does promise His presence and help. When Moses wavered, God promised, "I will help both of you speak and will teach you what to do" (Exodus 4:15b); "I am the Lord, and I will bring you out from under the yoke of the Egyptians. I will free you from being slaves to them, and I will redeem you with an outstretched arm and with mighty acts of judgment. I will take you as my own people, and I will be your God. Then you will know that I am the LORD your God, who brought you out from under the yoke of the Egyptians. And I will bring you to the land I swore with uplifted hand to give to Abraham, to Isaac and to Jacob. I will give it to you as a possession. I am the LORD" (Exodus 6:6-8). Repeatedly throughout the account, God reminds Moses of the promises and re-asserts God's faithfulness to lead and provide. As the community entered the wilderness, God's presence led the way as a pillar of fire during the night and a pillar of cloud during the day (Exodus 13: 21-22). As Joshua assumed leadership following Moses' death, God's promises remained firm. God reminded Joshua, "Be strong and courageous. Do not be terrified; do not be discouraged, for the LORD your God will be with you wherever you go" (Joshua 1:9). As a Serving Leader, remember that you are fully equipped to Run to Great Purpose by the God who created you; who calls you; and who sends you into the Kingdom's mission field. If you rely on your own strength and limited resources, you will falter. As you allow the Holy Spirit to fill and fuel you, you will run and not grow weary, you will walk and not faint (Isaiah 40:27-31).

In Lewis Carroll's Alice's Adventures in Wonderland, Alice meets the Cheshire Cat sitting in a tree as she travels an unknown path. Alice begins a conversation with the Cat this way:

> "Would you tell me, please, which way I ought to walk from here?"
> "That depends a good deal on where you want to get to," said the Cat.
> "I don't much care where," said Alice.
> "Then it doesn't matter which way you walk," said the Cat.

Pastor and author Andy Stanley says, "If you aim at nothing, you'll hit it every time!" Is your church or organization walking aimlessly toward a nebulous goal, or are you running purposefully toward a clearly articulated, God-inspired vision?

Remember, God promises to be your pillar of cloud by day and pillar of fire by night.

✝ Theological Foundations

Personal Purpose

Purpose is fundamentally an identity issue. Faced with unrelenting demands (both internal and external) and pressures to perform and excel, leaders often circumvent the foundational work of self-discovery and jump right into tasks and responsibilities. The "tyranny of the urgent[4]" commands our attention and distracts us from focusing on goals. Meaningful outcomes may be generated, **but it is easy to confuse busy with purposeful.** Leaders can only truly Run to Great Purpose when they have authentically walked the path of self-discovery.

Dr. Chris Hardy and Dr. Elizabeth Wourms developed a schematic (figure 1) for the curriculum of a 3-part formation experience called The Equipping Leader[5]. The diagram's flow (below) suggests that the pathway of self-discovery begins with honest, searching questions regarding the God who created us and calls us into service. Grounding our identity in Christ liberates us from bondage to external forces that contribute to a false identity. At the point of authentic self-discovery, people are in a position to explore issues of being. How do we live a life of worship, so that our very lives bring glory to God? What are the attitudes and behaviors that contribute to sustainability for leadership? How has God uniquely designed

---

4   Charles Hummel penned his classic essay, "Tyranny of the Urgent" in 1967. It is available through InterVarsity Press, Downers Grove, IL and on various Internet sites.

5   For more information about this course, please contact Elizabeth Wourms. Contact information is found at the back of the book.

and shaped each of us through spiritual gifts, talents, passions, abilities, and life experiences; and how does that uniqueness position each of us for the specific niche to which God calls? To what practices and spiritual disciplines must we attend in order to continue growing and maturing as disciples of Christ throughout our lifetime? As leaders engage these issues of being, then and only then are they truly positioned to address key questions regarding vocation. such as, what is God inviting and calling me to **do**? Articulating and carrying out a personal mission statement, or statement of purpose, is a matter of doing, but this exercise is predicated on a strong foundation of being. We dare not put the cart before the horse.

The Equipping Leader's Self-Awareness: Ontological Flow from Being to Doing

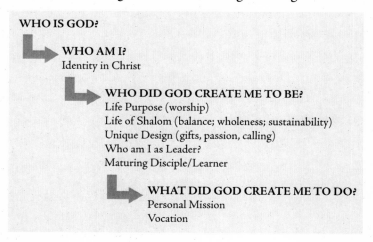

WHO IS GOD?

WHO AM I?
Identity in Christ

WHO DID GOD CREATE ME TO BE?
Life Purpose (worship)
Life of Shalom (balance; wholeness; sustainability)
Unique Design (gifts, passion, calling)
Who am I as Leader?
Maturing Disciple/Learner

WHAT DID GOD CREATE ME TO DO?
Personal Mission
Vocation

God fearfully and wonderfully made you, as the psalmist declared. There is no one else on earth who is exactly like you. You are uniquely fashioned and gifted by the Creator. God has given you physical attributes, an intellect, a personality, talents and abilities, and spiritual gifts. You are also formed by the culture in which you were raised and in which you currently live, and by the communities of people of which you are a part.

The Apostle Paul tells us, "Just as each of us has one body with many members, and these members do not all have the same function, so in Christ we who are many form one body, and each member belongs to all the others. We have different gifts, according to the grace given us" (Romans 12:4-6a). Paul expands this body metaphor in his first Corinthian letter. Regarding spiritual gifts he writes, "Now to each one the manifestation of the Spirit is given for the common good" (1 Corinthians 12:7). This theme is echoed elsewhere in Scripture. "Each one should use whatever gift he has received to serve others, faithfully administering God's grace in its various forms" (1 Peter 4:10). These Scriptures affirm that God does indeed give spiritual gifts to the Body of Christ through each unique member. Spiritual giftedness is part of a person's "divine design."

Another way in which you are unique is your personality. Your personal preferences, your drives, impulses, values, motives, needs, and the way you think, perceive, conceptualize, understand, feel, comprehend and make sense of things all flow out of your personality. Scholars and researchers have studied personality typing and have produced frameworks within which to conceptualize and characterize personality types. One of the most famous is the Myers-Briggs Type Indicator (MBTI). Another approach to personality typing is the DISC.

As a child of God, your life has purpose and meaning. God's care of and delight in God's creation is evident throughout the Scriptures. The church confesses this truth. The Westminster Catechism begins:

Q. What is the chief end of man?
A. Man's chief end is to glorify God, and to enjoy him forever.[6]

This inherent purpose—established in our very being as humans—derives itself from the Creator. Why do human beings exist? We exist to glorify God—this is our purpose. The Apostle Paul writes, "In him [Christ] we were also chosen... in order that we... might be for the praise of his glory" (Ephesians 1:11, 12). That we might be—that we might exist—for God's glory; this is our purpose as human beings. What incredible words of life! Serving Leaders embrace the wonder of this reality and seek opportunities to pour into others this hope-filled elixir. **No higher privilege of leadership exists than to speak these words to another person, "Your life has great meaning and purpose."** In a world that drains hope and life away, Serving Leaders invite people to see themselves as their Creator does— uniquely and wonderfully made; full of purpose and potential.

Since our purpose for existence is to glorify God and enjoy God forever, how do we live purposefully? The answer to this question speaks to each person's specific, God-ordained life mission. Your unique, personal design includes the combi-

---

6   The Constitution of The Presbyterian Church (USA), Part I Book of Confessions (Louisville, KY: The Office of the General Assembly, 1994), 181.

nation of your God-given characteristics and attributes; your particular passion; your leadership, personality, learning, and change styles; plus those formative experiences molded in culture and community. These characteristics and attributes—your uniqueness—help to form your identity as a leader and influence the ways in which you live out the leadership role in your current context of ministry.

Your life mission represents a template of purpose, or a stated plan of action as to how you will live your purpose "out-loud." Why are you here on this planet at this time? Your unique design informs your life mission, but it does not define it. Realize that your life purpose is bigger than both your design and your mission. Your life purpose describes the very reason for being. As human beings our purpose is to glorify God.

If purpose answers the "why?" question, then mission answers the "what?" question. What is it that you are called, specifically, to do with your purpose-filled life? We glorify God as we "offer our bodies as living sacrifices;" Paul says this posture is our "spiritual act of worship" (Romans 12:1). Worship-filled living that glorifies our Holy Creator includes spiritual disciplines, corporate worship, and a multitude of behaviors, attitudes, and actions. Knowing and living out your personal life mission is a key component of purposeful worship-filled living.

For many, this mission relates to their vocation or job. The word vocation derives from a Latin word vocare, which in essence means calling. Literally, vocare means to respond to a heard voice. As the voice of the Creator calls, what direction does God issue to you? Given your specific divine-design, what are you uniquely created and called to do? Reflect.

_____

_____

_____

_____

_____

As a leader in the church, you have articulated a "call to ministry." Within that broad, generic understanding, what is the heartbeat of your unique and focused call?

_____

_____

_____

_____

_____

Notice that your job is not the same thing as your mission. Once you reach clarity regarding what it is that you are uniquely designed and called to do, then jobs become a means toward that greater end (the mission) not an end in and of themselves. The mission is always larger than a job, position, or piece of work. Laurie Beth Jones, author of The Path, warns, "To confine the entire sum of your personality and gifts within the boundaries of your current job is to put yourself in the precarious position of losing your sense of identity when your job changes."[7]

---

7   Laurie Beth Jones, The Path: Creating Your Mission Statement for Work and For Life (New York: Hyperion, 1996), 9.

Your mission is always bigger than your relationships and roles, too. Perhaps your current role is pastor, or ministry leader. How does your role as pastor or ministry leader help to fulfill your overarching mission?

_____

_____

_____

_____

_____

Is your life mission currently being "swallowed up" or eclipsed by a broad job description? Which "plate," among the multitude of spinning plates in your life, contains the heartbeat of your call—the essence of your personal life mission?

_____

_____

_____

_____

Jones clearly defines the objective of a mission statement, "Having a clearly articulated mission statement gives one a template of purpose that can be used to initiate, evaluate, and refine all of one's activities."[8] Articulating a well-focused mission statement can help to provide the destination on the map toward which your whole life navigates. Each step along

---

8   Ibid, XI.

the way, each piece of the journey, takes you toward the goal and focuses you in a particular direction. A mission statement helps you to name and own your unique function within the Body of Christ. **What is the primary thing that God would use you to accomplish for the sake of the Kingdom and the world? Identifying this compelling "reason why" will better enable you to Run to Great Purpose.** What could be more compelling than God's plan and purpose for your life?! We encourage you to schedule some time on your calendar to develop your personal mission statement.

Organizational Purpose

Serving Leaders carry both the privilege and the responsibility of lifting up the banner of purpose for their team or organization. This purpose, or "reason why," must be so clear, so compelling, and so grand that everyone catches the vision and becomes motivated to join in and run after it. Often during college football games, a member of the cheer squad runs across the field or around the perimeter track holding a huge team flag out in front. This flag, or banner, is usually so huge that it's a wonder the person holding it can even carry it aloft, let alone run with it. Emblazoned with the school colors and logo, the flag symbolizes school pride and spirit and unites fans with their team in pursuit of victory. The Serving Leader should lift up purpose with the same clarity and fervor; the people should unite with equal zeal.

Clarity regarding personal purpose forms an essential prerequisite for organizational or team purpose. Leading people into unchartered territory proves difficult. When a leader understands and owns personal vision and life purpose, then that leader is in a position to invite others onto a similar journey of discovery. When each team member attains clarity and ownership around their personal mission and purpose, then the team can ready itself for the kinds of robust conversations that generate a powerful and God-inspired vision and purpose for the team itself. Often when leaders and team members lack clarity around personal purpose, they wind up mismatched and ill-suited for the positions they occupy. As Jim Collins made clear in his book, Good to Great, leaders must ensure that the right people are in the right seats on the right bus[9]. Frequently, in struggling organizations, it is the leader who is in the wrong seat, perhaps even on the wrong bus. Alignment between personal purpose and job/ministry description leads to the formation of high-capacity ministry teams. These **high-performing teams demonstrate alignment of personal and team purpose.**

Author and poet David Whyte informs our understanding of Run to Great Purpose. As he ponders what it means to chart a course and navigate effectively in one's work, Whyte likens it to following a star. He writes, "I thought of the old Latin root of the word desire, meaning de sider, of the stars. To have a desire in life literally means to keep your star in sight, to follow a glimmer, a beacon, a disappearing will-o'-the-wisp over the horizon into someplace you cannot yet fully imagine... The presence of the star does not excuse us from the difficult territory through which it is guiding us.[10]" Much like the biblical

9 Jim Collins, Good to Great, (New York: HarperCollins, 2001), 41ff.
10 David Whyte, Crossing the Unknown Sea: Work as a Pilgrimage of Identity, (New York: Riverhead Books, 2001), 78-29.

wise men, who followed God's star with a sense of unwavering purpose, Serving Leaders pursue a similar beacon. God leads faithful people into a God-ordained mission. **Serving Leaders become the navigators, the ones holding the compass, for their team or organization**. Often the Serving Leader becomes the one holding the spotlight, shining the way forward along the path. But always, it is God who provides the North Star—the larger directional marker; and it is God who fills leaders with godly desire.

Whyte adopts the poet William Blake's understanding that dedication to purpose is a firm persuasion. Whyte maintains, "To have a firm persuasion in our work—to feel that what we do is right for ourselves and good for the world at the exactly same time—is one of the great triumphs of human existence... To have a firm persuasion, to set out boldly in our work, is to make a pilgrimage of our labors, to understand that the consummation of work lies not only in what we have done, but who we have become while accomplishing the task.¹¹" Life and work come together in a passionate conversation—one in which heart, mind, and soul find voice and seek to both learn from and inform work. Out of this conversation, clarity of purpose emerges. Serving Leaders create space for these life-giving conversations to take place, both for individuals within themselves and for groups within the workplace.

---

11 Ibid, 4-5.

The Unique and Wondrous Paradox

Jennings and Stahl-Wert identify the Serving Leader paradox inherent in Run to Great Purpose as, "To do the most possible good, strive for the impossible." Sustain the self's greatest interest in pursuits beyond self-interest. Tragically, pursuing selfish interests and chasing a personal "pot at the end of the rainbow" are deeply ingrained tendencies in the human species. Particularly in Western society, we are inundated with external cues and messages, both overt and subconscious, seducing us on toward personal gain. Competing, coveting, and climbing characterize life's chase. The one who accumulates the most money, status, and possessions wins the race. The lure of achievement and accumulation plagues even faithful Christ-followers who seek to live lives of humility, selflessness, and generosity. What does it really mean to sustain one's greatest interest by engaging things beyond self-interest? What steps can we take to center ourselves in that worldview and adopt that lifestyle?

"Delight yourself in the LORD and he will give you the desires of your heart," the Psalmist says in chapter 37. At first glance, it appears that if we make God our delight that he will grant our personal wishes and desires. That's a dangerous interpretation, however, as it reduces God to a "genie in a bottle," an entity that exists to perform at the whim of the summoning person. As human beings, we exist to fulfill God's plans and purposes, not the other way around. As we delight in God and grow in our relationship with Him, He will give us desires—God will place desires in our heart that coincide with God's Kingdom purposes. Those desires become things that bring God glory and that demonstrate love for God and love for neighbor. Those desires become activities and pursuits that work for reconciliation, for peace, for justice. Those desires become avenues to sustain the self's greatest interest in pursuits beyond self-interest. Then we are better able to bless others with the words of the psalmist, "May [God] give you the desire of your heart and make all your plans succeed. We will shout for joy when you are victorious and will lift up our banners in the name of our God. May the LORD grant all your requests" (Psalm 20:4-5).

Twentieth-century writer and Christian apologist G.K. Chesterton observed, "How much larger your life would be if your self could become smaller in it!" Chesterton lifts up the paradox that characterized the life mission of John the Baptist. John recognized, "I am not the Christ but am sent ahead of him... He must become greater; I must become less" (John 3:28-30). John "lived out loud" a life of great purpose. He faithfully and boldly witnessed to the Kingdom of God and the arrival of the Messiah. John was not "less than" in any way shape or form; he was not a "nobody." He learned the key to running to great purpose, however. John realized that he needed to decrease in order that Christ might be lifted up in his life.

Ambition pales in comparison with purpose; **ambition is the anemic, sickly cousin to purpose.** The Apostle Paul writes, "Do nothing out of selfish ambition or vain conceit, but in humility consider others better than yourselves. Each of you should look not only to your own interests, but also to the interests of others. Your attitude should be the same as that of Christ Jesus…" (Philippians 2:3-5). In many respects it's easier to pursue ambition because it's our human default. Pursuing selfish ends comes naturally. As Whyte observes, ambition ironically clouds our vision, it hides our ability to see the stars; it takes away our God-given compass. As Serving Leaders, laying aside ambition becomes a first step toward running to great purpose. Ambition need not disappear completely (a healthy dose of ambition is a good motivator) but it must be held in check. As Whyte so helpfully illustrates, it is desire that informs a leader's conversation between self and world and fuels the passionate pursuit of purpose. As we allow God to provide desire as a gracious gift, then we become better able to lead our people in running to great purpose together.

Serving Leaders redefine "success" and develop new benchmarks that go way beyond productivity, numbers, and quantitatively measured outcomes. **Success becomes predicated on helping people within the organization to clarify identity and a sense of personal purpose and facilitating the team or organization to clarify who they are and what they are called to be and do collectively.** Successful outcomes focus on achieving the greater good together and encouraging, equipping, and releasing people to live abundant lives, serving passionately in areas that match their gifts and skills. Success as a Serving Leader has more to do with a legacy of people-development than a legacy of achievement characterized by plaques on the wall. What kind of legacy are you positioning yourself to leave?

As you navigate your personal crossing, remember that God

is at work within you "to will and to act according to his good purpose" (Philippians 2:13). As you leave selfish ambition behind and live in the freedom of God's wondrous paradox, you do so not in your own strength but with the grace, strength, courage, and conviction that only God can provide.

"But we have this treasure in jars of clay to show that this all-surpassing power is from God and not from us. We are hard pressed on every side, but not crushed; perplexed, but not in despair; persecuted, but not abandoned; struck down, but not destroyed. We always carry around in our body the death of Jesus, so that the life of Jesus may also be revealed in our body."
(2 Corinthians 4:7-10)

Key Behaviors and Practices

Following are some key behaviors and practices that you might consider adopting as you seek to more fully embody the Serving Leader Powerful Action, Run to Great Purpose. After reading this chapter, you may be thinking, **HOW** do I become a leader who runs to great purpose? We hope you find some helpful suggestions here. You may also find it beneficial to discuss your key learnings and "ah-ha's" with a trusted mentor or coach. S/he can assist you in considering behavior modifications, encourage you to take risks, and challenge you to stretch outside your comfort zone.

* Spend time in prayer, Scripture study, and reflection around identity in Christ
* Assess personal giftedness, skills, aptitudes, passion, abil-

ities, leadership style, change style

* Discern and develop personal mission statement

* Lead team and/or organization to paint a clear picture of organizational identity

* Lead team and/or organization to discern and articulate a clear, concise, and compelling vision and mission (organizational purpose)

* Revisit team and/or organizational mission during team meetings and re-cast vision (at least quarterly)

* Develop creative and diverse means and media through which to broadly communicate the organization's mission and its urgency so that the mission becomes a determiner of organizational culture

* Encourage each member of the team/organization to articulate a personal mission statement

* Discuss and celebrate as a team the ways in which each member's giftedness contributes to the team/organization's specific mission

* Empower each member of the team to own an essential piece of the mission; build roles and responsibilities into each member's job description accordingly

* Develop and implement a strategic plan with measurable benchmarks and outcomes; develop accountability structures to ensure that the plan is carried out

* Frequently remind team members of their personal "reason why;" frequently remind team members of the organization's "reason why"

* Celebrate each person's contribution to the "reason why" during annual performance reviews

* Model gifts-based and passion-fueled service for the members of your team/organization by finding your unique niche and staying focused within a narrowly defined job description
* Know what is "yours to do" (and what is NOT yours to do) and set appropriate and realistic boundaries around those roles and responsibilities

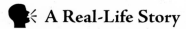 A Real-Life Story

By Wally Martinson, founder of The Nehemiah Foundation in Springfield, Ohio

The Nehemiah Foundation

I live in Springfield, Ohio. A number of years ago, Newsweek magazine called us "the All-American city." Near the crossroads of two major midwestern interstates, Springfield is in the demographic center of the country and really looks like what you might envision as a postcard "Anytown USA." McDonald's agrees, because it does food testing here.

But I had a growing concern for my city. As a Christian, family man, banker, and para-church worker, I saw that all was not as it seemed to be on Main Street. It's been said that people don't change unless they are in pain. Along with some fellow Christians from different churches, we began to feel the pain of a number of area social concerns—the rising number of out-of-wedlock births, divorces, drug users, people on welfare, health issues such as childhood obesity, etc. There were some city efforts going on to address a number of these challenges, but we began to feel a bigger vision was necessary.

What to do? We began with prayer. As a small group of 10–15 people, we courageously named ourselves the "Taking Our City for God" group, and we began to gather on a regular basis to share our concerns for our city and to pray. And this was our simple prayer: "Lord, we don't know what to do…We need **Your** vision." The group grew to about 200 people over the course of a year.

At the end of that year, Reid Carpenter, President of the Pittsburgh Leadership Foundation, came and spoke to us. His challenge was right to the point: "So after all this prayer, what are you going to do?"

We went to Pittsburgh and saw his model of addressing the needs of the city. We came back ready to get into the water.

We formed a steering committee of 18 very different Christians (Protestants, Catholics, Pentecostals, etc.) and I was tapped to be the Executive Director. Though diverse in some points of theology (initially I did not think we could agree on where to go to lunch much less what we believe), we were united around a bigger vision of Jesus and our community, and we were totally dependent on Jesus to lead the way.

And that He did. The first thing we did was ask 100 local leaders from different sectors (mayor, police chief, school principal, etc.) this question: "What are the top three problems in our community?" We sorted these answers into three basic categories: 1) breakdown of the family, 2) racial and economic division, and 3) moral bankruptcy of kids. These became our areas of focus.

We formed a board, The Nehemiah Foundation, based on the Old Testament city-restorer, Nehemiah. We formed a ministry model, a "bottom-up" approach that believed changed individuals leads to a changed city. Rather than reinventing the wheel, we first identified people in the community God was already using to bring effective solutions, and we simply supported them through prayer and financial support. We also did some investigation and looked at some "best practices" nationally and brought these ideas back to Springfield, feeling free to adopt/adapt them to fit our situation. We prayed for God to send new leaders to lead these initiatives. We never felt we could do it all. We simply prayed that God would help us find the right people to provide leadership, and then the resources to support them.

God did it. I could tell you story after story of His pieces being put into place. For example:

* A former school counselor started a ministry for juvenile delinquent kids, resulting in a drop in the recidivism rate and a huge cost savings for the city
* A county commissioner asked us to create a new program for getting people off welfare. We adopted a program from North Carolina that has helped over 1000 people get back to work.
* The Welfare Department asked us to create a program to help reduce the divorce rate. We found a great program in Tennessee and God directed someone to come to us with a passion for preventing divorces. The Marriage

Resource Center was established that over the last five years has helped reduce divorces in our city by 25%.

* A school administrator contacted us asking if we would partner with the school district in utilizing a federal grant to create "safe schools and healthy students." This grant ended up funding 11 full time employees who created "on ramps" for the community (including local churches) to "merge" into the "heavy traffic" at each of the city elementary schools. Six years later, community involvement is up over 300% in these schools.

In short, between 1992 and 2008, the number of projects addressing these social concerns in Springfield rose from three to 25, and the total budget rose from $60,000 to $2.5 million dollars. The leaders of these 25 programs, all funded in some way by the Nehemiah Foundation but operating on their own, now meet together six times a year to develop their own "bigger vision." They want to create benchmarks for infants though adults and a plan to produce mature Christian adults.

As for me, I am now on assignment in partnership with the Nehemiah Foundation. I'm trying to get pastors in Springfield together to rally around a purpose greater than themselves. We meet monthly and are building relationships as we ask the Lord: "What do you want us to do that we can't do by ourselves?" I pray God gives this group a vision so compelling that the churches of our community become truly united, just like what happened with fellow Christians addressing the social needs of the city.

I give God all the credit. He gave us the heart to notice the problems in our community, the desire to pray about them, and a vision to address them that united people across denominational lines. He gave us people to provide leadership, the resources needed, and effective programs to create, adopt, or adapt. And finally, He has given us much good fruit in the lives of many people who have seen His hand at work.

We discovered God could use us as the Body of Christ to help heal our community. We have not arrived, but are still in process. But we are running to great purpose together.

What can the Body of Christ do together that we cannot do separately?

Closing Thought and Questions for Reflection

God created us in His own image (Genesis 1:27), and gave us the responsibility to be good stewards of His creation and co-workers with Him in fulfilling His Kingdom purposes (Genesis 1:28, 2:15). As Serving Leaders, we have the opportunity to love God back by leading people to understand better who they are from God's point of view, and to fulfill what God's purpose is for their lives. This God-given who and what should be exciting and compelling for both leaders and for those being led!

Our leading has eternal significance, one way or the other. May you help many to Run To Great Purpose.

* How would you counsel Pastor John in the opening narrative?
* What is your greatest challenge to helping the people you are leading Run to Great Purpose?
* What's one thing that God would want to change in you in order to be a better Serving Leader in light of this chapter?

Upend the Pyramid

Jesus called them together and said, "You know that the rulers of the Gentiles lord it over them, and their high officials exercise authority over them. Not so with you. Instead, whoever wants to become great among you must be your servant, and whoever wants to be first must be your slave—just as the Son of Man did not come to be served, but to serve, and to give his life as a ransom for many."
(Matthew 20: 25-28)

Definition: Serving Leaders Upend the Pyramid of conventional thinking. They put themselves at the bottom of the pyramid and unleash the energy, excitement, and talents of the team, the business, and the community.

Paradoxes: You qualify to be first by putting other people first. You're in charge principally to charge up others.

"Humility is walking in the truth of who you are."
Saint Teresa of Avila

 Narrative

"The thing that frustrates me the most is the fact that we are supposed to be a Christian organization helping others, but we sure don't know how to help each other."

Jenny and Sue were on staff together at a well-known Christian non-profit in the city. They were riding home together and after a particularly hard day, Jenny just blurted out what they were both feeling. They had talked about their concerns before, in fact many times during many car rides home.

"What gets me," replied Sue, "is that we can be so publicly compassionate about the poor as an organization, but Mr. Harley doesn't have any idea how we are doing as employees. He just cares about the work, deadlines, and how we look compared to other non-profits... or better, how he looks compared to his peers."

"It really makes you wonder what leadership is supposed to look like," said Jenny. "I know we have a job to do, but it seems to me that God cares just as much about how we go about things as He does where we end up."

"I agree," said Sue as the car slowed to a red light. "But controlling people is a whole lot easier than loving them..."

Jenny thought about that for a moment and then asked "Why do the senior staff hide in their offices all day? Why can't they tell us what's going on more? Why can't they even ask our opinion some times? I feel like such a... such an 'employee' rather than a member of a ministry team."

Sue nodded her head and sighed in agreement. She pulled up into Jenny's driveway. "Well, see you tomorrow. Cheer up—it's only two more days until the weekend."

Jenny got out and replied through the open window, "Yeah... but after the weekend comes Monday, right?"

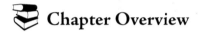 Chapter Overview

Serving Leadership characterized by self-less ambition, humility, and a priority on others' interests and goals flows from an attitude—a mindset—predicated on Christ and fueled by His indwelling Holy Spirit. Serving Leaders check their egos (Philippians 2:5-8); put others first (Philippians 2:3-4); charge others up (Ephesians 4:11-12); and function as catalysts for healthy growth and maturity in the Body (Ephesians 4:13-16). This chapter describes the Action, Upend the Pyramid. This Action serves to invert the traditional hierarchical pyramid of power and to locate the leader at the bottom, serving the majority who are at the top. Such a leadership posture goes against the grain of conventional thinking and wisdom, even within Christian circles. Upending the Pyramid is not as simple as reconfiguring your organizational chart to a more collaborative or team-based model. **To authentically Upend the Pyramid is to radically reconfigure one's heart, attitudes, mindset, and leadership style**. The "org chart" might remain a typical pyramid on paper, yet the "CEO" embodies an entirely different way of being and leading in ministry. The model is Jesus himself. We invite you to live into this paradigm with the humility and courage only Christ can provide.

📖 Biblical Foundations

The biblical witness upends the pyramid of conventional thinking. Serving Leaders Upend the Pyramid of conventional thinking and exercise biblical leadership. Serving Leadership flows from a biblical worldview characterized by humility, love, and grace; fueled by courage and confidence. Serving is both an attitude, and a lifestyle; it also represents a learned competency. Serving becomes a lifestyle as leaders prayerfully adopt the attitude and practice the competency. Serving ignites transformation through the indwelling Holy Spirit— transformation for both the one serving and for those whose lives are touched.

Building Up, Not Tearing Down

Scripture bears witness to extraordinary men and women who exemplify Serving Leadership. One of the most beautiful and poignant encounters is described in 2 Kings 2. As the Prophet Elijah's life and ministry drew to a close, God prepared to take Elijah up to heaven in a whirlwind. Elijah and his protégé, Elisha, traveled together, endured danger and hardship, prayed and served together, and cultivated an invested, intimate relationship. In short, they shared life. No doubt, Elijah became more than a teacher-mentor to Elisha; he became like a father to his mentee. These final days of Elijah's life must have been painfully bittersweet for both men as they celebrated all that they had experienced together, and prepared themselves for the agony of saying goodbye on death's doorstep. Elisha's raw emotion is evident in the text as he implores others not to speak of Elijah's impending death, and through his insistence that he remain with his mentor (2 Kings 2:3, 5, 6). Any of us who have lost a loved one, particularly a beloved mentor or parent-figure, can empathize with Elisha's situation.

What must Elijah have felt as he completed his travels, looked back on his life, passed the ministry baton to his mentee, and prepared to face death? His emotions must have run the gamut from joy to anguish, acceptance to fear, conviction to doubt. Time surely stood still in this final moment as past, present, and future crashed in on Elijah in an instant. Yet in this moment, suspended in time, Elijah upends conventional wisdom. His final act is not a grand display of prophetic brilliance, a deed to seal his ministry legacy and confirm his esteemed position. His final act is a grace-filled, loving act of service. We can almost imagine Elijah kneeling in front of his beloved Elisha and whispering, "Tell me, what can I do for you before I am taken from you?" (2 Kings 2:9). This profound and stunning question underscores Elijah's embodiment of Serving Leadership. Jesus' act of washing the disciples' feet as he prepared to be taken from them (John 13) is reminiscent of this tender moment between Elijah and Elisha. Elijah's final desire was that he might serve his protégé one more time, that he might invest in him, that he could empower him, and that he would release his potential. Elisha asked for a double portion of Elijah's spirit. In a sense, Elisha declared, "I want to become what I see in you." Serving Leadership is infectious. Serving Leadership is the legacy of a life well-lived.

Elijah used his authority well. Christ Jesus used his authority well. As the Apostle Paul closes his letter to the Corinthians, he illustrates the proper use of authority. "We are glad whenever we are weak but you are strong; and our prayer is for your perfection... that when I come I may not have to be harsh in my use of authority—the authority the Lord gave me for building up, not for tearing you down" (2 Corinthians 13:9,10). **The Lord gives leaders authority—it is a gift—for what purpose? For building up, not for tearing down.** The privilege and the paradox of Serving Leadership shines forth as God places leaders in positions of authority (builds leaders up) in order that they might be a channel of His grace to build others up. You, the leader, are in charge, principally to "charge up" others (Jennings and Stahl-Wert).

Paul develops this building-up leadership role in his letter to the Ephesians.

> *It was he who gave some to be apostles, some to be prophets, some to be evangelists, and some to be pastors and teachers, <u>to prepare God's people for works of service, so that the body of Christ may be built up</u> until we all reach unity in the faith and in the knowledge of the Son of God and become mature, attaining to the whole measure of the fullness of Christ.*
>
> *Then we will no longer be infants, tossed back and forth by the waves, and blown here and there by every wind of teaching and*

by the cunning and craftiness of men in their deceitful scheming. Instead, speaking the truth in love, <u>we will in all things grow up into him who is the Head</u>, that is, Christ. From him the whole body, joined and held together by every supporting ligament, <u>grows and builds itself up in love, as each part does its work</u> (Ephesians 4:11-16) [emphasis added].

God gives leaders as people-gifts to the Body of Christ. God gifts leaders to the Body in order that they might be equippers of God's people. God ordained this equipping role of leadership in order to build up the Body. **Equipping Leadership is Serving Leadership**. God gives leaders to the Body, not for the purpose of establishing hierarchy, not for the purpose of creating "professional" ministers, not for the purpose of developing those people to the exclusion of others. God builds leaders so that those leaders can build-up others! The result of people-development is growth in love, unity in the faith, knowledge of Christ, maturity, and fullness in Christ. The Message translation renders verse thirteen, "until we're all moving rhythmically and easily with each other, efficient and graceful in response to God's Son, fully mature adults, fully developed within and without, fully alive like Christ." What leader wouldn't want to experience those phenomena in their local fellowship? Author/leader Sue Mallory describes it this way, "When the church is healthy, she dances!"[12]Indeed it is God's design for you and your congregation. It all begins when leaders become intentional about using their authority well so that they can build others up.

---

12 Sue Mallory, The Equipping Church: Serving Together to Transform Lives, (Grand Rapids, MI: Zondervan, 2001), 25.

(Visit www.johnstahlwert.com/TSL for podcast #2 on "Why We Invest in the Development of People.")

Becoming a Servant

Paul exalts the Serving Leadership of Jesus in the beautiful Christ-hymn of Philippians 2. Paul sings:

> *Your attitude should be the same as that of Christ Jesus:*
> *Who, being in very nature God,*
> *did not consider equality with God something to be grasped,*
> *but made himself nothing,*
> *taking the very nature of a servant,*
> *being made in human likeness.*
> *And being found in appearance as a man,*
> *he humbled himself*
> *and became obedient to death—*
> *even death on a cross* (Philippians 2:5-8)!

Jesus Christ embodies Serving Leadership in a way that no human can ever approximate. The King of Kings and Lord of Lords, the Second Person of the Trinity, took on our human nature and became a servant[13]. This lifestyle and attitude are too amazing, too incomprehensible for words, and yet God

---

13 Serving Leadership differs from Servant Leadership in that it is both an attitude and a lifestyle. Theories of Servant Leadership provide a foundational skeleton from which to study servanthood, but Serving Leadership puts "flesh on those bones" in an Incarnational, embodied fashion. Serving Leaders exemplify three primary roles: Servant/Coach (Matthew 20:26-28), Teacher/Challenger (John 5:19-20), and Co-Creator (Ephesians 4:22-24). Jesus embodies all three and indeed they are wrapped up in his identity.

invites us to adopt them (Philippians 2:5). Serving Leadership is indeed both a mindset and a way of life. Serving can become one's worldview. Paul describes the lifestyle in the preceding verses:

> *If you have any encouragement from being united with Christ, if any comfort from his love, if any fellowship with the Spirit, if any tenderness and compassion, then make my joy complete by being like-minded, having the same love, being one in spirit and purpose. Do nothing out of selfish ambition or vain conceit, but in humility consider others better than yourselves. Each of you should look not only to your own interests, but also to the interests of others.* (Philippians 2:1-4)

God calls Serving Leaders away from selfish ambition toward **humility**. A humble posture makes possible the kinds of behaviors that build others up, that demonstrate a right use of authority. A lifestyle of Serving Leadership characterized by humility, and a priority on others' interests and goals, flows from an attitude—a mindset—predicated on Christ and fueled by His indwelling Holy Spirit. Serving Leaders check their egos (Philippians 2:5-8); put others first (Philippians 2:3-4); charge others up (Ephesians 4:11-12); and function as catalysts for healthy growth and maturity in the Body (Ephesians 4:13-16).

Notice that humility does not involve loss of self. On the contrary, authentic humility bears witness to a fully alive self. The "self-emptying" of Christ (Philippians 2:7) is frequently misinterpreted by scholars and readers of Scripture alike. We are not to conclude that Christ, through his Incarnation, emptied himself of something (becoming less than), but rather that Christ poured Himself out for the sake of others, becoming a servant. Jesus speaks of the path to life in the Kingdom of God as a giving up of one's life in exchange for receiving the life of Christ. As we lay down our lives for the sake of the Gospel, as we give up self, God does not call us to use up self. Receive this important distinction. Too often, loss of self becomes the high price of ministry for those in full-time service. Jesus lifts up the tension between sacrifice and abundant life with startling clarity.

> *"If anyone would come after me, he must deny himself and take up his cross and follow me. For whoever wants to save his life will lose it, but whoever loses his life for me and for the gospel will save it. What good is it for a man to gain the whole world, yet forfeit his soul?"* (Mark 8:34b-36) (cf. Matthew 16:24-26)

Sometimes in their zeal to serve, leaders sacrifice self on the altar of servanthood. Jesus' words ring true when applied to the demands of ministry, too. What good is it for a man to gain a "successful ministry," yet forfeit his soul? Many leaders wind up on this altar of sacrifice because they lack a firm understanding and ownership of their identity in Christ. Clarity regarding identity in Christ positions believers and leaders alike for resiliency and abundance in life and relationships; and prevents work, title, or position from becoming definers of identity. Humility combined with the self-confidence that comes from a relationship with Christ and the courage and faith that He provides makes possible the kind of pouring out of self that is truly life-giving for others and regenerative for the one serving. **A clear identity in Christ provides the necessary bedrock upon which the 5 Powerful Actions of Serving Leadership may be established.**

 (Visit www.johnstahlwert.com/TSL for podcast #3 on the subject of "Identity in Jesus Christ.")

Humility

As Jesus invited his disciples into a Serving lifestyle, he put forth the startling paradox of the humility that Paul later described. "The greatest among you will be your servant. For whoever exalts himself will be humbled, and whoever humbles himself will be exalted" (Matt. 23:11, 12).

What is your personal definition of humility? Describe a humble person.

_____

_____

_____

_____

_____

_____

Let's be honest, cultivating an attitude of humility in leadership is often difficult. We're conditioned for personal achievement and advancement. Where does humility show up in your leadership? Where is it lacking? Reflect.

_____

_____

_____

_____

_____

_____

The Apostle Paul offers encouragement, stating, "for it is **God** who works in you to will and to act according to his good purpose" (Philippians 2:13, emphasis added). As we surrender more fully to Christ's Incarnational presence in our lives, then His humility and His servanthood shine through us. Think about times in your life when you have sensed His Spirit informing your attitude and servanthood, and contrast those with times that you wound up serving in your own strength and effort. What were some of the differences in your experience? In others' perceptions of your leadership?

_____

_____

_____

_____

_____

_____

Humility is often misinterpreted in Western culture. People understand humility as "meekness," or "weakness." True humility differs radically from both self-deprecation and false modesty. Either putting oneself down or playing a charade that one is really not as gifted as others—both stances miss the mark. We need not think ill of ourselves, engage in self-degrading practices, or cover our pride with a veil of feigned modesty. The model is Christ, whose self-emptying was in fact a fulfilling of his true vocation (Philippians 2:7, 8). Christ humbled Himself by resisting the temptation to follow an easier calling—one that would have denied His authentic self. No hint of self-deprecation exists in Jesus' attitude or behavior. His embodied self-giving does not forbid taking an interest in one's own affairs. It simply stands in stark contrast with a selfish preoccupation that ignores or prevents interest in the lives of others. Far from weakness, **authentic humility reflects a quiet confidence in one's identity in Christ.** St Teresa of Avila described humility as "walking in the truth of who you are." The humble leader exhibits keen self-awareness, and lives and moves in the abundant freedom that self-knowledge affords.

An old country western song proclaimed, "Oh Lord, it's hard to be humble when you're perfect in every way!" We cannot be truly humble apart from God's grace. Humility without grace is pride in disguise. Humility without grace becomes a badge of honor. If you want to know how humble I am, just ask me! Left to ourselves, we base our identity on externals and locate our self-worth in our own supposed self-righteousness, or "works." When our identity is grounded in Christ, then we experience the freedom to form an authentic self-understanding based on God's grace and received as pure gift. Only then is authentic humility possible. Only then are we free to walk in the truth of who we are, and able to embody biblical humility. Only then do we come alive in our creative orientation as we become more fully available to the breath of the Spirit filling and fueling our vision and guiding our outcomes. In a posture of authentic humility, the Serving Leader flourishes as co-creator with God in God's missional activity, and invites others to do the same.

Ministry leaders often find themselves in prestigious places simply by virtue of their position. Ministry becomes one more profession in which those at the upper echelons receive greater honor, status, and privilege. God's Word advises, "The fear of the Lord teaches a [person] wisdom, and humility comes before honor" (Proverbs 15:33). Many ministry leaders unconsciously seek status and position under the guise of servanthood. Status, position, affirmation, recognition, and accomplishment fuel hidden needs. These leaders unintentionally become Super-Servants—elevated to a pedestal of superior service. God provides a pathway to greatness, and it is the way of humility. It begins with grace. James illustrates this glorious pathway.

> "But he [God] gives us more grace. That is why Scripture says: 'God opposes the proud but gives grace to the humble.' Submit yourselves, then, to God. Resist the devil, and he will flee from you. Come near to God and he will come near to you. Wash your hands, you sinners, and purify your hearts, you double-minded. Grieve, mourn and wail. Change your laughter to mourning and your joy to gloom. Humble yourselves before the Lord, and he will lift you up" (James 4:6-10).

Notice the "bookends" of this passage: God gives more grace

and He will lift you up! The pathway of humility involves submission, resisting evil, drawing near to God, confession and repentance. Humility envelopes all of these disciplines, and humility becomes the gracious outcome. Peter echoes this exhortation, "Humble yourselves, therefore, under God's mighty hand, that he may lift you up in due time. Cast all your anxiety on him because he cares for you" (1 Peter 5:6-7).

By now, you may be saying to yourself, I am a humble person. I've got this part under control. The following brief assessment may challenge some of your closely held assumptions. Reflect prayerfully on the statement and supporting prompts, and ask God to shine the light of revelation into your hidden places for the sake of your personal transformation.

Rate yourself on a scale of 0—5, with 0 being "never" and 5 being "always."

> "Successful ministry involves personal success and advancement."

0   1   2   3   4   5

You likely rated yourself a 1 or 2. But what if...

* God raises up someone else to lead **your** vision.
* You're the most qualified, but someone else is invited to lead the project.
* You did all the work, but someone else gets the credit.
* You seldom receive thanks or recognition, but others do.
* You find it easy to make unilateral decisions without in-

viting others into the process.
* You frequently use "I" or "me" language when speaking of the ministry to which you're called.

I (Elizabeth Wourms) I had the privilege of helping to start a non-profit organization that serves the city of Dayton, OH. The organizational launch was at a juncture where many exciting possibilities were beginning to emerge, and potential players were starting to come to the table. It appeared that others might be about to run with pieces of **our** vision. During a conversation with one of my mentors, he said, 'Elizabeth, you shine the brightest when it doesn't matter who does the work as long as the work gets done.' His words penetrated to a recessed area in my psyche and my soul—a dark place where hidden motivators reside and inform behavior. I realized in that moment that it **did** matter—it mattered a lot and I wanted the credit for all the sweat equity, sacrifice, and tears that I'd invested in the process. God used that occasion to invite me into greater humility. I grew as a Serving Leader that day.

> *"Therefore, as God's chosen people, holy and dearly loved, clothe yourselves with compassion, kindness, humility, gentleness, and patience. Bear with each other and forgive... And over all these virtues put on love, which binds them all together in perfect unity"* (Colossians 3:12-14).

The Serving Leader text describes the Action, Upend the Pyramid. This Action serves to invert the traditional hierarchical pyramid of power and locate the leader at the bottom, serving the majority who are at the top. **Despite the leader's best in-**

tentions and the organization's commitment to upending the pyramid, this phenomenon will never occur without two key elements: humility and confidence. The humility-confidence dyad forms the pivot upon which the traditional pyramid flips. Without humility, the upended pyramid may be a drawing on a page or a stated goal, but it will never be embodied in the life of the leader and modeled for others in the organization. Lacking confidence, the leader lets down her guard or loses hope, and the pyramid immediately reverts back to the hierarchical orientation because that posture is "safe"—it is familiar; it affords the illusion of control and competence. Without firm identity in Christ and a fierce resolve in the power of the Holy Spirit, leaders may be able sporadically to flip the pyramid and demonstrate Serving Leader tendencies; but when backed to the wall, leaders who lack that inner Spirit-fueled fortitude will default to whatever orientation and leadership posture is congruent with their human nature and innate hard-wiring[14].

Pastor-Author Leonard Sweet lifts up the need for Christian leaders to embody a humble-confidence and confident-

---

14 The insight and understanding around humility as a central aspect of upending the pyramid was developed during The Equipping Leader, Part 2 course during the Fall 2007. My colleague, Dr. Chris Hardy, and I (Elizabeth) developed a 3-part, 30 hour Intensive course as an off-shoot of our work in the doctor of ministry program at United Theological Seminary. It was during one of our class discussions on Serving Leadership that one of the participants offered the helpful insight that humility might be the pivot upon which the Pyramid turns. I'm indebted to Dr. Hardy and our students for helping to flesh out these concepts and painting a relevant picture of what it means to Upend the Pyramid. For more information on the Equipping Leader course, please feel free to contact me through the information at the back of the book.

humility[15]. Sweet's playful semantics brings the centrality of Christ into clear focus. **Humility says "it's not about me;" confidence says "it's all about Christ and His work in and through me."** Blogger Bill Cochenour offers helpful commentary. He writes,

> *"What if self-confidence limits what God wants to do? What if being self-confident is a little like the boy with the 5 loaves and 2 fish (Mark 6:30+) being confident he could feed a family of three? He could feed that family but Jesus intended to do something 5,000 times bigger. Worse yet, what if self-confidence actually gets in the way of what God wants to do? Besides, how solid is your self-confidence, really? Does it run deep all the time? I am beginning to believe that self-confidence is the antithesis of God-confidence because the sources for each are mutually exclusive. One is rooted in pride and the other in humility. One is dependent on strengths we can muster on our own. The other is dependent on the power of God in our weakness.[16]"*

Blogger Mark Batterson joins the conversation. He suggests,

> *"Self-confidence is two inches deep. I don't care about it. I don't want it. It typically undermines my raw dependence upon God anyway. It's unhealthy. It's unholy. There is a higher, deeper and truer confidence that comes from God. Think of it as <u>God-confidence</u>. And it's the byproduct of two things. First, God-con-*

---

15 I (Elizabeth) heard Len Sweet discuss this concept of humble-confidence/ confident-humility during Leadership Network's webinar, The Nines, on September 9, 2009. http://thenines.leadnet.org/

16 http://cogun.com/_blog/Bill_Couchenour/post/What_is_the_source_of_ your_confidence/. Site accessed on June 27, 2010, 7:57AM.

fidence is a byproduct of humility. The more you [sic] humble yourself before God the more favor you expect. It sanctifies your expectations and it builds a holy confidence that God is in control. Humility is the way we stay out of the way of what God is doing. <u>Holy Confidence is confidence that finds it's locus in Christ alone.</u> The confidence for salvation. The confidence of favor. The confidence for miracles. The confidence for grace. Second, God confidence is the byproduct of authority. We grossly underestimate the authority that is ours by virtue of the fact that we are "in Christ." He has given us "all authority." As long as we are functioning in the will of God, all things are possible. If that doesn't give you confidence nothing will.[17]"

The Apostle Paul summarizes this notion of humble-confidence/confident-humility in his stirring declaration, "I can do everything through him [Christ] who gives me strength" (Philippians 4:13). Without Christ and left to our own devices, our efforts are anemic at best and sanctimonious at worst. With Christ, we live and move and have our being in Him, with the confidence, grace, and authority that He provides. Serving Leadership flows out of this relationship with Christ.

Humility—walking in the truth of who you are—coupled with confidence through the Holy Spirit, generates courage and strength for the journey. A humble posture demonstrates total surrender to God's will and to God's ways and belies authentic dependence on God for strength and stamina. Christ declared, "I am the vine; you are the branches. If a [person]

---

17 http://www.evotional.com/2010/03/holy-confidence.html. Site accessed on June 27, 2010 at 8:03AM.

remains in me and I in him, he will bear much fruit; apart from me you can do nothing" (John 15:5). In our nothingness, in our utter and complete dependence, God provides courage and confidence. That is why the Apostle Paul was able to resound, "being confident of this, that he who began a good work in you will carry it on to completion until the day of Christ Jesus" (Philippians 1:6). The courage that only God can provide echoes throughout the biblical witness. Just as God poured out courage upon Joshua, God faithfully fuels leaders today. "Be strong and courageous, because you will lead these people... Do not let this Book of the Law depart from your mouth; meditate on it day and night, so that you may be careful to do everything written in it... Be strong and courageous. Do not be terrified; do not be discouraged, for the Lord your God will be with you wherever you go" (Joshua 1:6-9).

 (Visit www.johnstahlwert.com/TSL for podcast #4 on "Upend the Pyramid.")

Keeping It Real

As a Serving Leader, name some **practical** steps you can take to Upend the Pyramid in your own life as a leader.

_____

_____

_____

_____

_____

_____

_____

As a Serving Leader, name some practical steps you can take to cultivate humble-confidence and confident-humility in your life so that the pyramid won't revert back to a hierarchical leadership posture?

_____

_____

_____

_____

_____

_____

_____

Read Matthew 20:16, 25-28; 23:11-12. How might the message in these verses help you to Upend the Pyramid?

_____

_____

_____

_____

_____

_____

_____

God's Power; Your Weakness

Finally, the great paradox of Serving Leadership is summed up in the biblical reality of power made perfect in weakness. Indeed, the paradox undergirding Upend the Pyramid (you're in charge principally to charge up others) is predicated on this biblical worldview. God reveals this paradox powerfully and persuasively:

> *"Has not God made foolish the wisdom of the world? For since in the wisdom of God the world through its wisdom did not know him, God was pleased through the foolishness of what was preached to save those who believe. Jews demand miraculous signs and Greeks look for wisdom, but we preach Christ crucified: a stumbling block to Jews and foolishness to Gentiles, but to those whom God has called, both Jews and Greeks, Christ the power of God and the wisdom of God. For the foolishness of God is wiser than man's wisdom, and the weakness of God is stronger than man's strength. Brothers, think of what you were when you were called. Not many of you were wise by human standards; not many were influential; not many were of noble birth. But God chose the foolish things of the world to shame the wise; God chose the weak things of the world to shame the strong. He chose the lowly things of this world and the despised things—and the things that are not—to nullify the things that are, so that no one may boast before him. It is because of him that you are in Christ Jesus, who has become for us wisdom from God—that is, our righteousness, holiness and redemption. Therefore, as it is written: "Let him who boasts boast in the Lord. When I came to you, brothers, I did not come with eloquence or superior wisdom as I proclaimed to you the testimony about God. For I resolved to know nothing while I was with you except Jesus Christ and him crucified. I came to you in weakness and fear, and with much trembling. My message and my preaching were not with wise and persuasive words, but with a demonstration of the Spirit's power, so that your faith might not rest on men's*

wisdom, but on God's power." (1 Corinthains 1: 20b—2:5)

A Serving Leader takes up Paul's cry, "I resolve to know nothing except Jesus Christ and him crucified!" **In order to Upend the Pyramid, you must die. Period.** You must die to self and selfish interests; you must die to selfish ambition and vain conceit; you must die to the ways of the world and external pressures to conform; you must die. In that moment of death to self, God brings resurrection and lifts you up so that you might walk in newness of life. Walk this way—receive God's life, resolve to abide in Christ and to allow Him to mold you into the Serving Leader that He invites you to be.

✝ Theological Foundations

Serving and Lording
Read and reflect on the following verses:

> *"Jesus called them [the disciples] together and said, 'You know that the rulers of the Gentiles lord it over them, and their high officials exercise authority over them. Not so with you. Instead, whoever wants to be great among you must be your servant, and whoever wants to be first must be your slave—just as the Son of Man did not come to be served, but to serve, and to give his life as a ransom for many'"* (Matthew 20:25-28).

In this passage, serving stands in stark contrast to lording. These verbs can be both attitudes and behaviors. Attitude informs behavior, and behavior reinforces attitude. Reflect on these concepts in light of your own life and experience.

Compare and contrast the attitudes and behaviors of serving versus lording:

Attitude of Serving:

_____
_____
_____
_____
_____

Attitude of Lording:

_____
_____
_____
_____
_____

Serving Behavior:

_____
_____
_____
_____

Lording Behavior:

_____
_____
_____
_____

Notice that Jesus' teaching on servanthood comes in response to the mother of James and John requesting places of prominence for her sons in Christ's Kingdom. James and John have clearly forgotten the serving paradigm that they have already witnessed. Mark describes the scene. "As soon as they [disciples and Jesus] left the synagogue, they went with James and John to the home of Simon and Andrew. Simon's mother-in-law was in bed with a fever, and they told Jesus about her. So he went to her, took her hand and helped her up. The fever left her and **she began to wait on them**" (Mark I: 29-31, emphasis added). This woman's response to Christ's transforming influence in her life was serving. James and John witnessed this encounter, but the implication was lost on them. In response to His love and grace, Christ calls us to humble service in His Kingdom, not pursuit of status and position.

Forsaking status and position is a foreign concept in today's world. It was just as alien to ancient Hebrew and Greek thought. Even though the Old Testament writers understood the concept of service and the command to love one's neighbor, their thinking was limited to charitable acts. Diakonia, the term translated as service, or ministry, is not found in the Septuagint (the Greek translation of the Old Testament). Judaism in the time of Jesus proclaimed social responsibility, particularly to the poor and widows, but these populations were served primarily through the giving of alms, or offerings, not direct service. Lowly service was considered beneath the dignity of a free person.

As you lead God's people, what influences pressure you to seek status, advancement, or position? Think about both internal and external pressures.

_____

_____

_____

_____

_____

_____

_____

Jesus defines diakonia through his personhood and his actions. Throughout the New Testament, service/ministry becomes a term denoting loving action for one's neighbors, which is derived from divine love. Jesus said, "I am with you as one who serves" (Luke 22:27). Ministry also describes one outcome of koinonia, or authentic Christian community.

The fellowship of the common meal is foundational to the New Testament concept of diakonia (Acts 2:42-47). The agape meal (the precursor for the Sacrament of the Church that we know as Eucharist, Communion, or the Lord's Supper) was central to intimate fellowship, worship life, the rich caring for the poor, and sharing life, strength and possessions. The spiritual and physical diakonia of giving and receiving takes place in the acknowledgement of Christ's ultimate sacrifice. Service, therefore, contains a sacramental nature. Service springs from gratitude for Christ's redeeming sacrifice and from coming together as His Body to commune together in Him. Our oneness in Christ as members of His Body sparks our service. Service is not an individual pursuit. Service is essentially communal.

Christ tells us (Matthew 20) that those who desire greatness must become servants, and those who want to be first must become slaves. The Greek term translated slave is doulos. A doulos was a person who was subject to another, or in submission to another. As we saw in Philippians 2, "Your attitude should be the same as that of Christ Jesus: Who... made himself nothing, taking the very nature of a servant (doulos)..." Christ's counter-cultural attitude and action instills radical value in a doulos. Unconditional love expressed through service is the heart of the Incarnation. As Christ is incarnate in us, then we embody the character of a doulos.

Humans have always been obsessed with the illusion that we can make or maintain our own life and freedom with reference to ourselves and in our own power (self-actualization). The ancient Greeks regarded this type of individual aggrandizement as the highest form of freedom. The Bible reveals that type of freedom as sin. Self-actualization without purpose, or selfish ambition, becomes a false god. Christ sets us free from the slavery to sin and liberates us to be slaves in Him. Paradoxically, Christ's liberation invites us into a divine love-relationship that expresses itself through service. In this love-relationship, life and freedom are made possible through the Lord, the Giver of Life, who invites us into the co-creator relationship in the power of the Holy Spirit. Surrender replaces self-actualization in Serving Leadership, as the leader yields and submits to God's authority and leadership.

In what ways is this type of radical, biblical servanthood in direct opposition to the prevailing mores and values of 21st century Western society?

_____

_____

_____

_____

_____

_____

Do you find the terms serving and leadership to be contradictory? Why or why not? Explain.

_____

_____

_____

_____

_____

_____

The Super-Servant

As a leader in ministry, you are no doubt recognized as a servant. In pursuing your call to ministry, serving and service are inherent in your vocation. No doubt serving is part of the culture of your church or organization. Reflect on the following questions:

How would the people in your congregation/organization broadly define serving or service?

_____

_____

_____

_____

_____

_____

How do they, themselves, expect to serve? Do they regard themselves as servants?

_____

_____

_____

_____

_____

_____

_____

Think about how the members of your congregation or organization view you in your role as leader. How do the people
expect you to serve them?

_____

_____

_____

_____

_____

_____

_____

In the space below, visually depict your church's/organization's
model of serving or service. What does service look like? What
kinds of behaviors are demonstrated? Who is serving whom?
A model is simply a visual representation of the "real thing."
Think creatively about how to describe your congregation's (organization's) embodiment of service using pictures, diagrams,
symbols, a story board, etc. Use as few words as possible.

_____

_____

_____

_____

_____

Most people who articulate a vocational call to ministry express a strong desire to serve others. In fact, service is a primary driver and motivator for ministry leaders willing to give their lives in the service of others. Indeed the biblical call to serve is clear and non-negotiable.

Serving others as an aspect of ministry becomes disempowering, however, when the servant performs tasks for another person that s/he could accomplish for her/himself. Sometimes in a desire to "help" or "fix," the servant only fosters a position of neediness in the one being "served." Granted, occasions exist in which we are called to "give a person a fish" as an act of service in order to meet an immediate need. As Serving Leaders, however, God calls us to "teach people to fish" and to be catalysts for others' growth and discipleship by releasing gifts and potential. The Serving Leader is not focused on doing things **for** other people; the Serving Leader desires to partner **with** others in order to grow, serve, and thrive together.

Admittedly, over-functioning/under-functioning reciprocity stands in the shadow of servanthood. This phenomenon is one of several relationship patterns described by Bowen Family Systems Theory (BFST). Ministry leaders will find BFST helpful, not only in understanding their family of origin and the ways in which those relationships have shaped their lives, but the theory also informs congregational life as a "family system." Many ministry leaders easily fall into the over-functioning/under-functioning reciprocity with members of the congregation, and with the congregation as a whole. In this "see-saw" relationship, we often observe the following:

The over-functioner:

* Knows the answers
* Does well in life
* Tells the other what to do, how to think, how to feel
* Tries to help too much
* Assumes increasing responsibility for the other
* Does things for the other he or she could do for self
* Sees the other as "the problem" (where issues or anxiety exists)
* Demands agreement, bringing on "groupthink"

The under-functioner:

* Relies on the other to know what to do
* Asks for advice unnecessarily
* Takes all offered help, needed or not, becoming passive
* Asks the other to do what he or she can do for self
* Sees self as "the problem"
* Is susceptible to "groupthink"
* Eventually becomes symptomatic (anxiety, illness)[18]

---

18 For a helpful and concise summary of BFST, see Roberta M. Gilbert, MD, *The Eight Concepts of Bowen Theory: A New Way of Thinking About the Individual and The Group*, (Falls Church & Basye, VA: Leading Systems Press, 2004). Bulleted list above adapted from p. 18.

Many leaders who ascribe to the theory of "servant leadership" wind up trapped in patterns of over-functioning. The lure of the "ministry darkside" is to become "super-pastor" or "super-leader." Just as destructive, however, is the lure to be a "super-servant." **Super-Servants fall into a syndrome of behaviors in which their desire to serve others dwarfs their call to invite and equip others to live their own call to service.** In the "super-servant syndrome," the leader winds up doing most or all of the work—the service—while the recipients become passive, atrophied, and dependent upon the leader. In her zeal to serve, the Super-Servant winds up robbing those served of the life-giving opportunity to live their own biblical invitation to exercise discipleship through service. The Super-Servant becomes a martyr, sacrificed on the altar of super-servanthood. In this syndrome, the people elevate the Super-Servant to an idolatrous pedestal, celebrating her/him for exceptional service, but all the while growing increasingly stagnant in their own journey with Christ. Within this framework, servant-hood becomes a badge that we wear proudly, proclaiming to the world what great servants we are. If a leader isn't careful, Upending the Pyramid can cause the pendulum to swing too far toward this idolatrous place. Sound ludicrous?

Examine your own calendar. How many hours per week do you devote to your ministry?

_____ Hours/week.

If you are in full-time, vocational ministry and you work more than 50 hours/week, examine your motivation. Have you fallen into the trap of "super-servanthood?" Do you feel as if you are always "on the clock" for ministry? Would your family say that they have lost you to the "work of the ministry?" Reflect.

_____

_____

_____

_____

_____

_____

_____

Super-servants resemble the pagan shaman. The connotation of a shaman is one who mediates between the people and a deity, and who possesses supernatural powers or abilities not available to ordinary people. The shaman occupies a superior rung on the "spiritual" ladder. You know you've become like a shaman, a Super-Servant, when the people understand you to be the only one capable of performing a certain service, or the only one who should perform a certain service. The people's expectations drive your performance.

An example in the church is hospital visits. Do the people feel that they have been served if someone from the congregation comes to pay a visit, or do they only feel served when the pastor/priest visits? Reflect.

_____

_____

_____

_____

_____

_____

_____

Jesus Himself was confronted with this same temptation. The opening chapter of Mark's Gospel highlights many of Jesus' healing miracles (see Mark 1:21-34). Mark continues his account, "Very early in the morning, while it was still dark, Jesus got up, left the house and went off to a solitary place, where he prayed. Simon and his companions went to look for him, and when they found him, they exclaimed: 'Everyone is looking for you!' Jesus replied, 'Let us go somewhere else—to the nearby villages—so I can preach there also. That is why I have come'" (Mark 1:35-39). The crowds, and to a certain degree even his disciples, had already labeled Jesus a "Super-Servant." They already expected that He would continue to serve and give as they demanded. The disciples' mild reprimand, "Everyone is looking for you!" implies "Come on, get busy serving!" Christ exhibits true Serving Leadership in His affirmation of His call to proclaim the Good News of the Kingdom. Miracle working was part of His ministry, but Christ was clear on His call to preach. He resisted the people's demands that He become shaman-like.

How about you? Are you clear on God's specific and focused call to service? Have you zeroed in on the "heartbeat of your call?" Or, do you just busily serve in whatever capacity is warranted or according to the demands and expectations of others? Reflect.

_____

_____

_____

_____

_____

_____

_____

Christ also modeled Serving Leadership in His commitment to abide in His Father's presence in order to receive super-natural resources through the Holy Spirit for guidance and direction. Serving Leaders create margin in the midst of their service for solitude and prayer. Reflect on the margin or lack thereof in your own life.

_____

_____

_____

_____

_____

_____

_____

As you read and reflect, you may be saying to yourself, "I have no issue with lording. I'm not seeking status; I'm just living my call to serve." The hidden irony for many in full-time min-istry, however, is that serving unconsciously becomes lord-ing when serving becomes the leader's idol. **Serving God and others can become the god you serve**. Consider Ken. He is a pastor who has fallen into over-functioning in ministry. He never takes a day off and rarely sleeps. Ken maintains, "God wakes me up every night and calls me to prayer and to wrestle with issues facing the ministry." While this may be true occasionally, God's desire is that people would experience health and wholeness—shalom. God would never call a leader into an unhealthy lifestyle. This pastor, in his desire to serve God's people, has made serving into an idol. He is sacrificing himself on the altar of the god of "service". His thinking about and/or doing "ministry" around the clock is evidence that serving has become a consuming and controlling force in his life. As this pastor becomes better able to follow Jesus' example, as evidenced in Mark 1:35-39, he gains clarity regarding what it is that is uniquely his to do, and discovers his motivators for over-functioning. Then he will be able to enter the pathway of healthy, Serving Leadership.

Sometimes leaders mask an unconscious need for control under the guise of servanthood. How about you? Do you have a need to control the various aspects of ministry and service within your sphere of influence in your congregation or organization? Reflect.

_____

_____

_____

_____

_____

_____

_____

To what extent are you able to equip and release others to carry out their unique serving opportunities and leadership roles without (unintentionally) micro-managing? Reflect.

_____

_____

_____

_____

_____

_____

_____

Serving Leadership invites a different paradigm. **Serving Leaders serve the organization above self, serve the mission even more, and serve people the most.** Serving Leaders become catalysts for transformation, not only in their own lives as they seek daily to experience sanctification and growth in Christlikeness, but also in the lives of those with whom they serve. Serving Leaders desire to see others realize their greatest potential and to succeed in whatever God calls them to be and to do. Serving Leaders invite those whom they serve to be participants in the process of moving toward greater health and vitality. **People-development lies at the heart of Serving Leadership, over against any desire to simply perform tasks or accomplish service.**

 (Visit www.johnstahlwert.com/TSL for podcast #5 on "Servanthood as Idol.")

Mini Assessment

Rate yourself on the following statements, with 0 being "never," and 5 being "always."

I desire to attain positions of greater authority and/or position throughout my ministry career.

0   1   2   3   4   5

I would tend to pursue ministry opportunities only if there was a position or paycheck attached.

0   1   2   3   4   5

I desire "better" positions that are "higher" in the organizational structure.

0   1   2   3   4   5

My ministry is primarily confined to what is outlined in my job description.

0   1   2   3   4   5

I view my performance evaluation as key to professional advancement.

0   1   2   3   4   5

If I'm honest, I often think to myself, "ministry would be great if it wasn't for the people."

O   I   2   3   4   5

When I close my eyes and think about my ministry, the
first thing I see in my mind's eye is responsibilities and
tasks.

O   I   2   3   4   5

Ministry often feels like a weight on my shoulders or a
heavy burden.

O   I   2   3   4   5

I feel anxious when it seems like I'm not accomplishing
anything.

O   I   2   3   4   5

Add up your ratings _____. If you rated yourself at 30 or
higher, your service may be more about your own striving and
success than authentically serving and supporting God's people. Find a trusted confidante and discuss what you see in this
assessment and what you're discovering about yourself and
Serving Leadership through this resource.

Personal Theology

At this juncture, we encourage you to pause for serious reflection on your personal theology of ministry/service. If you are
a member of the clergy or a paid staff member in a ministry
setting, this exercise proves particularly critical. Your self-
understanding as a leader must be informed by your theology
of ministry, and vice versa. How do you understand yourself,

both in terms of your being (identity) and your doing (role, functions, position)? What is your theology of ordination? Of the Priesthood of Believers? Of Baptism and its function in the life of a believer? Describe your ecclesiology (your view of the Body of Christ and of Church and its structures and governance). Your personal theology (consciously or sub-consciously) forms the lens through which you view your church or organization, and becomes the driver for your adoption (or ultimately rejection) of Serving Leadership. Personal theology influences the development of the authentic humility and confidence necessary to Upend the Pyramid.

Priest and author Henri Nouwen sketches a most humbling description of a Christian leader. Nouwen suggests that the Christian leader must beware of the temptations to be relevant, popular, and powerful. Only in a willingness to be irrelevant, in surrendering self-sufficiency, in reclaiming one's "unadorned self," and in gaining a willingness to be vulnerable, can Christian leaders truly give and receive love.[19] The wonderful paradox in this attitude toward Christian service is that leaders can be both irrelevant and truly self-confident at the same time, because of Christ's love. Nouwen argues convincingly that if, in our Christian leadership, leaders aim to be spectacular, the lost will not recognize that they come in the Name of Jesus. Jesus calls leaders to lead and minister not as professionals, but as vulnerable brothers and sisters who are willing to follow Jesus' example of Serving Leadership. Finally, rather than a struggle to exert power and authority, Christian

---

19 Henri Nouwen, In the Name of Jesus: Reflections on Christian Leadership, (New York: Crossroad, 1989).

ministry is in large part being led in order to lead. Leaders must allow God to lead them so that they can lead the people to whom they are called. **Controlling people is often easier than loving them**, but God calls leaders to the challenge of love and to the Cross, not to control.

Leaders live out a "Redemptive Theology" or an "Incarnational Theology" when their lives demonstrate congruence of belief and action. Such leaders seek to bring the reality of Jesus into the lives of all those whom they encounter—living life in such a way that others see the love of Jesus and are drawn to the Gospel through their witness. Disciples of Jesus are called to live a joy-filled life so that the lost will wonder, "How can I have what they have?" Leaders become Jesus' love, his hands, his feet, and his Words. This is theology that matters; this is life worth living; this is Serving Leadership.

Because many congregations have bought into a theology of the church that elevates the value and status of the clergy and church staff, in comparison to the rest of the People of God, a biblical theology of holy vocation is needed to correct this inequity. Moses declared such a word to Israel:

> "For you are a people holy to the Lord your God. The Lord your God has chosen you out of all the peoples on the face of the earth to be his people, his treasured possession. The Lord did not set his affection on you and choose you because you were more numerous than other peoples, for you were the fewest of all peoples. But it was because the Lord loved you and kept the oath he swore to your forefathers that he brought you out with a mighty hand

and redeemed you from the land of slavery, from the power of Pharaoh king of Egypt" (Deuteronomy 7:6-8).

God chose a particular people to be a treasured possession and the purpose of this election was redemption and freedom from oppression. God intends that the People of God be free—free to live out their created design and divinely ordained purpose as treasured ones.

A Serving Leader sets the captive people free to live out their unique and particular function within the Body of Christ. God set believers free in order that they might serve in God's Kingdom as priests! God's people are saved in order that they might be in relationship with the Living God as a holy nation, as the Body of Christ. Out of that covenant relationship, believers receive identity as children of God and that identity gives expression to a community's life together. Disciples of Christ have been set free in order that they might participate together, within the holy nation, as God's priests and ministers.

The People of God are currently in bondage in many settings. The ordained ones, the clergy, are enslaved to an understanding that ministry is "all about me," that as "CEO" of the organization that they are not only "in charge," but fully responsible for carrying out the work of ministry. The non-ordained ones, those commonly referred to as laity, are enslaved to an understanding that the ministry belongs to the clergy and that they are "just" volunteers whose sole purpose is to help the clergy carry out their responsibilities and tasks.

The powerful Exodus metaphor of the Hebrew Scriptures provides a foundation for God's transforming work in the lives of God's followers. An exodus, a transformational experience, involves a leaving behind (death), a wilderness experience (in between state/burial), and entrance into the Promised Land (resurrection). When church leaders have the courage to liberate the captives, they leave behind the old paradigm of institutionalized church, in which the clergy is responsible for the work of ministry and the laity merely observe or assist. Then they enter into the wilderness, in which a new way of being the church is embodied. The wilderness is a time of great turmoil, change, and angst as a congregation wrestles with what it means to cultivate a culture of Serving Leadership. The wilderness period involves a re-envisioning of corporate identity and a willingness to experience congregational transformation. Finally they enter the Promised Land when individuals and the entire congregational system experience transformation through the leading and refining of the Holy Spirit, and the Body of Christ becomes more fully incarnate.

As the Apostle Paul reflected on his ministry and service to God's people, he made a profound assertion. Paul's declaration forms the foundation for authentic Serving Leadership. Without tapping into this essential truth, it is impossible to embody Serving Leadership. Paul writes, "To this end [pursuing the call] I labor, struggling with all his [Christ's] energy, which so powerfully works in me" (Colossians 1:29). Paul labored and struggled in ministry, not in his own strength and limited resources, but with all of Christ's energy, powerfully at work in him. Christ promised, "But you will receive power when the Holy Spirit comes on you" (Acts 1:8). The Greek word translated power is **dynamin**, as in dynamite! Believers receive spiritual dynamite when they receive the Holy Spirit. In that defining moment, one's life pursuit becomes Christ crucified, and the joy-filled desire to share that sacrificial love with the whole world. Christ's energy, His life-giving, Resurrection power, is at work in you! Have you fully surrendered and yielded to it? Have you fully availed yourself to it? As you do, it will no longer be you who serves, but **it will be Christ who serves His people through you**. Paradoxically, then and only then, will you become a Serving Leader.

Previously, you depicted your congregation's model of service. Based on what you've learned about Serving Leadership and Upending the Pyramid, draw a model of service in the space below based on your new understanding.

_____

_____

_____

_____

_____

_____

_____

⌨ Key Behaviors and Practices

Following are some key behaviors and practices that you might consider adopting as you seek to more fully embody the Serv-

ing Leader Powerful Action, Upend the Pyramid. After reading this chapter, you may be thinking, **HOW** do I become a
leader who is able to successfully Upend the Pyramid? We
hope you find some helpful suggestions here. You may also
find it beneficial to discuss your key learnings and "ah-ha's"
with a trusted mentor or coach. S/he can assist you in chang-
ing your behavior, encourage you to take risks, and challenge
you to stretch outside your comfort zone.

Assess your personal Leadership Style.[20]

Assess your church's or organization's governance and/or
leadership structure. Think beyond your organizational chart.
How does the **culture** of your organization inform and dictate
"how things are done around here?"

* Does your organization embody a typical hierarchical or
  "top-down" leadership structure and practices?
* Does your organization embody a team-based, or collaborative approach to leadership structure and practices?
* How easy is it for grassroots initiatives to take off and
  flourish in your organization's culture?
* Are you intentionally and actively cultivating and releasing emerging leaders?
* Do leaders feel empowered to lead and serve without
  fear of micro-management?

---

20 A variety of assessment tools and resources exist. We recommend Who Am
I as a Leader? Loveland, CO: Group Publishing, 2006). This publication
is a self-contained training module designed to be a 4-hour session for
use with a team or larger gathering of people.

These are just a sampling of questions you might want to consider as you assess your organization's governance and structure.

Based on your assessments (both personal and corporate), what are 3 steps you can take to either begin to upend the pyramid in your organization, or to continue to maintain an upended pyramid?

1. _____

2. _____

3. _____

Key Behaviors exhibited by Serving Leaders who Upend the Pyramid:

1. Spend significant time each week in people-development (equipping and encouraging others is a practice built into the leader's calendar and to-do list). Incorporate people-development into the job description.

2. Consciously and prayerfully examine personal motives (particularly around power, authority, and control) on a continual basis.

3. Continually be asking yourself as a Serving Leader these questions:
    * How can I better serve the organization?
    * How can I better serve the mission/vision more?
    ▪ How can I better serve people the most?

4. Regularly seek feedback from others (peers, subordinates, supervisors, direct reports, other leaders) regarding whether or not "walk matches talk." In other words, if the Serving Leader believes that s/he Upends the Pyramid, do others perceive their attitude and behaviors as congruent with this Serving Leader posture.

5. Relate to volunteers not as "worker-bees" who are needed to perform tasks and enhance programs, but as people gifted by God and essential members of Christ's Body. Assist volunteers to connect with opportunities to serve that are good matches for their gifts and skills and guide volunteers to reflect upon their service so that service becomes a pathway for growth in discipleship.

6. Exhibit authentic humility, courage, and confidence through the indwelling Holy Spirit. (Regularly seek feedback from others, asking what evidence they see of these characteristics in your life.)

7. Prayerfully act on feedback received and make necessary behavior modifications as needed.

8. Seek coaching or mentoring for support, accountability, and encouragement.

9. Clearly articulate personal leadership style and authentically embody it. Maintain appropriate boundaries around time, calendar, and professional duties; balance work, family, and self appropriately.

A Real-Life Story,

By Todd Braschler, Todd Braschler Ministries in Witchita, Kan.

As a young teen, I loved canoeing in the Ozark Mountains in and near where I grew up in St. James, Mo. The Meramec River always offered a day of peace and cool water after a long day at work. Driving down the red dirt roads of Missouri en route to the bridge to launch our canoe, I often noticed a trickle of water that made a muddy rut in the road. One day, out of curiosity, I pulled my truck over to the side of the road and followed that trickle of water back into the woods. What a surprise to discovery a hidden spring, a natural flow of freezing cold, pure water bubbling out of the rocks and caves of the Ozark Mountains. What a joy it was to discover this gem in the heavy undergrowth of the woods. A refreshing, invigorating source of joy was hidden there in the rocks all those years until I found a way, better yet, took the time to stop and investigate the source of this stream across the road. That pretty well describes the experience I enjoyed while on staff at the Central Community Church of God in Wichita, Kan. the day I met Judy Smith (alias).

Shortly after receiving a call to join the staff at Central Community Church as an associate pastor in the areas of equipping, assimilation, leadership development and connecting ministry, it became very evident that there was little, if any, training options available for anyone desiring to grow in their ability as a leader. If you wanted any training of the sort, you were expected to travel to another church, another community, or watch a webcast at our church. There was no real strategy or plan offered to identify, develop or train leaders. I just couldn't stand by and watch incredibly gifted and called people with tremendous leadership potential simply sit in pews on Sunday morning and see these abilities invested in the world rather than ministry.

As a first step, we began laying out a vision for the kind of leaders we felt called to build. We asked the question, "If God had his way in our efforts to build leadership at this church, what would a leader focused and aligned in the center of God's giftedness and passion look like?" I purchased a video curriculum for leaders and began advertising a weekend retreat for anyone desiring to learn how to be that kind of God-anointed leader. This did not come without criticism mind you, as other pastors and leaders thought I was somehow luring their leaders away from their ministry to my own. On the contrary, I simply wanted to pour fuel on anyone desiring to grow in their leadership ability, and understand the role of a Biblical leader.

How exciting it was to see that first group arrive for this training, the first in many years. One participant who arrived that day was a middle-aged blonde—haired lady from our community. She was very sophisticated looking, as she made her way to the tables up front. Ironically, my oldest son, who was 12 years old at the time was also seated at that table. You can always tell who is the most confident in themselves in training sessions by who marches right to the front table to sit down. That was the case with this lady, who soon identified herself as a business professor at the local university. Her name was Judy, a single mother of 3 boys (2 off to college or grown, 1 son still in high school.) She was not single by choice, but forced into single parenthood as the result of an unfaithful husband. In an act of desperation, Judy pulled into the parking lot of our church some months back, and had begun, for her, a commitment to a church on a regular basis, for what seemed to be the first time in her life.

I was immediately struck and actually rocked back on my heels at times by responses to questions, very mature insight into leadership issues, and Judy's intentional investment in my son while they sat together with others at the front table of this conference. It was obvious from the start that she had received extensive training as a leader already, and that she saw herself as a leader. One thing I've learned over the years—in order to connect with true leaders, you must utilize the right bait. By bait, I mean this—leaders love to learn about leadership. Leaders thrive on the idea that if we grow in our ability to set direction, understand people, sense the potential or calling in people, and become incredibly focused at excavating that calling and potential, we as leaders in turn find a great sense of fulfillment. The correct bait to attract leaders to events and training turned out to be opportunities to equip and develop this gift in application to so much more than just ministry. That was Judy Smith spot on. She thrived in this setting, and I was determined to find out more.

In the months that followed, as I would challenge Judy in leadership opportunities, and as I heard more of her story, God began to open a door, a vision for Judy's leadership. In the months and years that followed as her walk with Christ and her leadership ability both grew, Judy became a co-teacher with me for the Spiritual Gifts discovery process of our church. We formed numerous other teams to care for people, and guide them through the journey of finding that unique place of ministry. We began a leadership lunch for anyone in our community that wanted to simply become a better leader. Churches and organizations and businesses began sending their employees to our church for a once-a-month lunch and a lesson on leadership. With Judy's leadership, we built a team of leaders who greeted, registered, served the meal, distributed the materials, and cared for those who walked into our church to learn about leadership. I watched her passion for the souls of people continue to grow, as well as the passion within those many team members we were leading and developing.

In 16 months, we saw over 600 people either affirmed of their current ministry opportunity, or led to discover ministry within their passion in a new and fresh way. We also saw that small beginning of a leadership lunch go from 17 people average to over 77 people attending each month. And upon my resignation 3 years later, and move to another full time opportunity in ministry, Judy eventually led both the team leading the teaching of Spiritual Gifts, and the leadership lunch team without my leadership. These two ministries continued to grow and strengthen for two more years following my departure due to Judy's leadership. If she hadn't remarried and moved away, these teams of people would still be leading what I would consider two of the most fulfilling elements of ministry I've personally ever been a part of.

As a young pastor, the opportunity to lead someone to Christ personally, to build a ministry, the chance to start and finish a project or responsibility brought great joy. It didn't take long to realize, however, that the joy in ministry was multiplied enormously when the same result was achieved by identifying, training and equipping leaders, watching them grow and stretch and risk, and turn themselves into disciples of Christ, hungry to serve him. My job, my role as the pastor of these endeavors quickly moved from the organizer, the teacher, the responsible party, the sole provider to the welcome team, the encourager, the provider, the "fanner of the flame" and the congratulator. Judy not only became a spiritual leader in addition to a professor and teacher, she influenced and challenged me in the areas of leadership and teaching that were areas of weakness for me.

Today I make a living teaching and speaking all over the country. We just celebrated our 10th year in full-time ministry in 2011, and I owe a lifelong debt to Judy Smith for what she taught me about teaching, creativity, and intentional investment in people. This experience also taught me to seek out those small signs of leadership potential in others, to use ministry to build and develop people, rather than use people to build and develop ministry. It taught me to stop the truck, get out of my schedule and agenda, and take a walk to follow what looks like an insignificant trickle of muddy water to discover a wellspring of refreshment, a surprise in the dense undergrowth of ministry and my personal life. Since then, my life is so much the richer for others like Judy whom God has brought across my path to stop and invest in to see and experience God's miraculous calling on those who will set aside career, rights and success to invest in people as He did.

Closing Thought and Questions for Reflection

As you can see, Upend the Pyramid is basically about attitude—having the same serving attitude as that of Jesus (Phil. 2:5). It is possible to do all the other Serving Leader Actions mechanically well, but if our attitude isn't Christ-like, then we can be laboring in vain from God's point of view. If our attitude is right, all the other Serving Leader Actions will flow out freely with a "want to" instead of a "have to." And God knows the difference.

* Who taught you about leadership? About serving leadership? Who are you/should you be teaching about serving leadership?
* Do you have the courage to ask the people you are serving if they think you are a serving leader like Jesus? Why or why not?
* What's one "pearl" you want to treasure from this chapter?

Raise the Bar

Jesus went up on a mountainside and called to him those he wanted, and they came to him. He appointed twelve—designating them apostles—that they might be with him and that he might send them out to preach and to have authority to drive out demons.

(Mark 3:13-14)

Definition: Serving leaders Raise the Bar of expectation by being highly selective in the choice of team leaders and by establishing high standards of performance. These actions build a culture of performance throughout the team, business, or community.

Paradoxes: To serve the many, you first serve the few. The best reach-down is a challenging reach-up.

"Intentional mediocrity is a sin."
Elton Trueblood

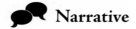 Narrative

As the new principal of Oakdale Christian School, Doug Smith was excited, yet a little anxious regarding his first all-staff meeting. The board had hired him to help revive the spirit and vision of the school, now in its 16th year. While teaching the past 12 years at a nearby community public school, Doug had achieved a Masters degree in School Administration, and this would be his first position as a school principal. He wanted to get off to a good start.

The meeting went well until Doug shifted gears and began to talk about raising the bar of expectation of teachers. Doug began, "As you know, we have a 16-year history as a school. From what I understand, the past four years have not been the best. Attendance and income have been on a slow downward trend. Each one of you probably has an opinion as to the cause of this. I think a good place to start is to re-examine our core values and what we expect from our teachers. I think—"

"I'll tell you the reason this school is turning south," interrupted Hal Morgan, one of the school's science teachers. "It's because the administration expects too much of us and we then have to decide what we can and cannot do. For instance—"

"For instance," blurted Melanie Blatos, a sixth-grade teacher, "you will say one of the core values is 'excellence,'—but how can we teach with excellence when we have to attend teacher meetings every week, prepare for all kinds of 'special school activities,' constantly record all our lesson plans on the school web-site for parents, chase after students who are missing homework, meet with parents who don't understand why their son or daughter didn't get an 'A' on the last spelling test, and deal with disrespectful students during our planning period?"

"And here's the kicker, Mr. Smith..." said a measured voice from the back of the room. Alice Greanleaf had been one of the original teachers and had the respect of the entire faculty. When Alice spoke, people listened. "The kicker is that we have heard this speech before from others like you. But why do the leaders of this school not submit themselves to the same core values they hold us to?"

The room got very still. All eyes swung back to Doug Smith for an answer.

Doug swallowed hard. This was not going to be as easy as he had hoped.

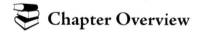 Chapter Overview

A recent Google search on the phrase "Raise the Bar" netted 6,150,000 hits! Clearly it is an often used metaphor. Track and field aficionados will instantly recognize the reference. In the high jump and pole vault events, the bar is set at consecutively higher levels as competitors successfully attain each level. The athletes constantly strive to clear the next highest level, thus improving their performance and advancing on toward a win. The one who attains the highest level of the raised bar wins. Stamina, skill, advancement, self-improvement, success, accomplishment—all are terms inherent in raising the bar. The phrase comes loaded with competitive edge; it invites us higher; it compels us farther; it never settles for second best. We live in a competitive world; we constantly face raised bars.

Raising the bar is, in essence, the pursuit of excellence. Ministry involves the pursuit of excellence as we seek to honor God and participate in God's Kingdom enterprises. How do we follow this noble pursuit without falling into the trap of selfish ambition and vain conceit (Philippians 2:3)? How do we balance exhorting people to live to their full God-given potential with the caution to be humble and unselfish? In this chapter we delve into the biblical paradoxes of power made perfect in weakness and the necessity of dying in order to live. For Serving Leaders, raising the bar is truly only possible as we fully embody our God-given position in Christ.

📖 Biblical Foundations

The Apostle Paul captures the essence of Serving Leadership, and particularly the competency, Raise the Bar, succinctly in his letter to the Church at Corinth. Paul admonishes, "Nobody should seek his own good, but the good of others" (1 Corinthians 10:24). Leaders demonstrate an ultimate concern for people and their greatest good as they invite others to attain full potential and strive for a higher level.

Challenging Reach-up
In their writing on Raise the Bar, Jennings and Stahl-Wert portray the wondrous paradox that captures the essence of au-

thentic helping, serving, and equipping: the best reach-down is a challenging reach-up. As we consider the biblical foundations for Serving Leadership around Raising the Bar, God invites us to remember our baptism. The Apostle Paul writes,

> *"Or don't you know that all of us who were baptized into Christ were baptized into his death? We were therefore buried with him through baptism into death in order that, just as Christ was raised from the dead through the glory of the Father, we too may live a new life. If we have been united with him like this in his death, we will certainly also be united with him in his resurrection"* (Romans 6:3-5).

Baptism reminds Christ-followers that the pathway to life begins paradoxically in death. No detours exist on this pathway in the Kingdom of Heaven. Death presents the sole life-giving option. As leaders offer a hopeful and life-giving reach-up, it is essential that they lay a proper foundation—a firm footing for the person being served and equipped. I believe Scripture compels us to consider the paradox this way: a challenging reach-up includes both a summons to die to self and an invitation to experience new life in the power of the risen Christ. In our zeal to offer the reach-up, if we only issue the invitation to life then we negate the possibility by our critical omission. God releases potential from the barrenness of a dormant seed. **The best reach-down begins with a call to die.**

The inherent danger in raising the bar is that we set the stage for people to experience one of two phenomena—either a sense of inability to measure up; or the perception

that serving involves a series of performance standards that one can attain by "trying harder." Many fall on the double-edged sword: discouragement leads to a form of works righteousness—always striving harder to attain the performance "holy grail." These people remain trapped in a vicious cycle of discouragement, striving, sense of failure; discouragement, striving, sense of failure… Reclaiming our baptism provides the means to avoid these extremes and the avenue toward meeting the raised bar. Two Scriptures beautifully illustrate this foundational truth.

You are likely familiar with Jesus' encounter with the "Rich Young Ruler" (Matthew 19:16-30; Mark 10:17-31; Luke 18:18-30). I invite you to pause in your reading to review the entire text; we pick it up here in Matthew's account at verse 21:

> *"Jesus answered, 'If you want to be perfect, go, sell your possessions and give to the poor, and you will have treasure in heaven. Then come, follow me.' When the young man heard this, he went away sad, because he had great wealth. Then Jesus said to his disciples, 'I tell you the truth, it is hard for a rich man to enter the kingdom of heaven… When the disciples heard this, they were greatly astonished and asked, 'Who then can be saved?' Jesus looked at them and said, 'With man this is impossible, but with God all things are possible.'"*

You have likely heard many sermons on this passage, and participated in Bible studies that considered this text. Often, the sermon or study focuses on the issue of personal sacrifice, and begs the question—what are you willing to give up in order to follow Christ? What are the things in your life that consume your focus and attention; those things that you cling to rather than being 100% "sold out" to our Lord? We are often exhorted to rid ourselves of earthly treasure in order to attain heavenly treasure. Inevitably, the question of "riches" and what constitutes "richness" accompanies an investigation of this passage. Ultimately, we feel sorry for this rich young man—if he could have just mustered the courage to part with his wealth—to do the right thing; then he could have been free to follow Jesus and find eternal life. We're also left feeling not just a little bit uneasy and perhaps a tad guilty and insecure, wondering what am I holding back? And, is it preventing me from entering into eternal life? I believe there is a more fundamental interpretation to this passage and it speaks directly to the principle, Raise the Bar.

The entirety of the biblical witness points to the finished work of Christ and our participation in Him by grace through faith, not by our works. Ephesians 2:8-10 states this truth succinctly, "For it is by grace you have been saved, through faith—and this not from yourselves, it is the gift of God—not by works, so that no one can boast. For we are God's workmanship, created in Christ Jesus to do good works, which God prepared in advance for us to do." Because Christ's work on our behalf was the Tri-une God's gracious plan from the foundation of the world, Jesus embodied this divine arrangement in every encounter and interaction. Therefore, to read the account of the "Rich Young Ruler" and to conclude that Christ was calling him to some legalistic course of action in order to acquire eternal life would be erroneous. His query, "Good teacher, what must I do to inherit eternal life?" (Luke 18:18) is the wrong question! "Do" and "inherit" are mutually exclusive concepts. Heirs typically are not required to jump through hoops in order to accept what is rightfully theirs as gracious gift. Yet Christ patiently entertains the "list game" with the young ruler. The two discuss God's commandments and the man's zealousness in keeping them. Since the young man felt assured of himself in his faithful law-abiding, Christ raised the bar: "If you want to be perfect, go, sell your possessions and give to the poor..." In this brilliant employ of hyperbole, Jesus sets the bar at an unattainable level. You can almost see the twinkle in his eye— ok, if you think you're perfectly law-observant, are you willing and able to follow it out to the "nth-degree?"

Or perhaps more realistically, I envision our Lord with tears of compassion and longing in His eyes (see Mark 10:21) because He so yearned for the young man to awaken to this conclusion and cry out in humble admission: "**I can't do that on my own!**" If the young man could have become broken to the point of that pivotal confession, then I imagine Christ kneeling in front of him, wrapping him in an ardent embrace, and drying the young man's tears of sorrow and repentance. I hear Christ whisper to him, "You're right, you cannot do it on your own and it's OK! You can cease striving and trying to be good and do right in your own strength; take my yoke upon you because it's easy, and learn from me and I will give you the strength and power you need to follow me as my disciple. Die to self; receive eternal life." Instead, the young man went away sad. This is one of the most poignant and tragic scenes in all of

Scripture. Eternal Life was standing right in front of him—the very thing he sought—but the young man failed to recognize his need to die to self and to embrace the gift of life that awaited him. He mistakenly believed he had to earn it by trying harder. In his pride, he could not admit to the Lord that he lacked the ability to work it out on his own. He needed a Savior—not just for his salvation but also for his discipleship. How many of us continue to play the part of the Rich Young Man in a similarly tragic scene because we persist in attempting to work out our discipleship and even our leadership on our own initiative?

Jesus' disciples missed the truth, too. After witnessing the encounter, they blurted out, "Who then can be saved?" (I would be surprised if there wasn't a "gee whiz" tacked onto that question somehow.) Jesus patiently admonishes, ("Don't you see?") "With man this is impossible, but with God all things are possible." ("You're right, no one can perfectly keep the law.") Peter argues, "We have left everything to follow you! What then will there be for us?" Peter indignantly plays the martyr, reporting the notches on his discipleship belt and he essentially says, "That rich guy wasn't willing to be totally sold out to you, Lord, but I sure am! I've got this service-thing down!"

In the ensuing verses, Jesus acknowledges that the path of discipleship does indeed require personal sacrifice, and those who sacrifice much will be rewarded. Ultimately, Christ gets to the crux of the matter, "But many who are first will be last, and many who are last will be first" (Matthew 19:30). In the paradox, Jesus paints the canvas for a Serving Leader's life. This irony becomes the essential ingredient in Upending the Pyramid, as well as for

Raising the Bar. The "rich man" in Jesus' story is anyone who be-lieves that s/he possesses the capacity for Christ-centered living, and indeed for Serving Leadership in and of themselves! It is so easy to become "rich" in self-assurance, in one's gifts, talents, and abilities, in one's educational background, in one's training and preparation. Indeed, trusting in self and self's abilities, and seeking one's own worth outside of God form the root of all sin. **Before a person can rise to meet a raised bar, s/he must first die—die to self and self's own interests and striving—and die to sin and become united with Christ in His death.** Death is the portal to life abundant and eternal; there is no other door. This door also marks the entrance into Serving Leadership. Just as a person cannot secure their own salvation or live as a disciple of Christ according to their own strength and initiative, **one cannot authentically function as a Serving Leader in their own strength and initiative**. A second Scripture text demon-strates this critical truth, as well.

The Apostle John illustrates the attitude and posture of a true disciple, and consequently of a Serving Leader. In his Gospel, John records Jesus' words,

> *"I am the true vine, and my Father is the gardener. He cuts off every branch in me that bears no fruit, while every branch that does bear fruit he prunes so that it will be even more fruitful. You are already clean because of the word I have spoken to you. Re-main in me, and I will remain in you. No branch can bear fruit by itself; it must remain in the vine. Neither can you bear fruit unless you remain in me.*

I am the vine; you are the branches. If a man remains in me and I in him, he will bear much fruit; apart from me you can do nothing. If anyone does not remain in me, he is like a branch that is thrown away and withers... If you remain in me and my words remain in you, ask whatever you wish and it will be given you. This is to my Father's glory, that you bear much fruit, showing yourselves to be my disciples" (John 15:1-8).

In verses 1-4, God the Father is the subject. I find great hope and encouragement in the fact that God prunes fruitful vines. If you've ever experienced pain, frustration, or disappointment in the midst of God's pruning (perhaps a particular ministry ended prematurely, maybe a funding source dried up, possibly your leadership was challenged) then find comfort in these verses. God prunes the fruitful vines—not the unfruitful ones—in order that they might grow to greater fruitfulness, ultimately for God's glory. (Note that the fruit-bearing is for God's glory, not for the glory of the branch!) Our Heavenly Father is a loving Gardener. God's work of pruning is a loving act—nurturing, caring, delighting—in a very intentional and deliberate manner. As we abide in Christ, we avail ourselves to God's delighting in us as He shapes us for His purposes.

When we think in terms of this metaphor, it's glaringly obvious that a branch removed from the vine cannot bear fruit. It's not only obvious—it's ludicrous to imagine that it could produce fruit! How could a branch that is cut off from its life source possibly thrive? And yet if I'm honest, I have to admit that I've lived much of my life working really hard to be fruitful in my own strength and limited resources. Oh sure, I've kept my faith, hope, and trust in God and even sought guidance and provision through prayer, but have failed to truly abide in the Vine. Why do I so often choose to become this lifeless picture:

when I have been given the gift of God in Christ to abide in the Vine and be fruitful?

As related in verses 5-8, Jesus' focus shifts from the Gardener to the disciple. In this passage, Christ makes the disciple's role and task crystal clear: the disciple is to abide. The term "abide/ remain" and its antithesis, "apart," occur six times in this short text, which serves to underscore and emphasize the directive. The Greek term that is translated "remain," or "abide" carries a sense of permanence. When one abides, she does not come and go—she dwells permanently. As Christians, we often fail to assume residence in the Vine; or we live and behave as if we were somehow disconnected from our Life Source. You are not homeless! Your permanent dwelling place is in Christ the Vine.

Startlingly enough, the disciple is not summoned to action, s/he is called to abide. Out of the abiding, flows the fruitfulness! **The problem with discipleship in many of our churches is that well-intentioned leaders exhort the people to live faithfully—to keep commandments and to exercise spiritual disciplines and to give generously and to serve sacrificially—but these leaders neglect to encourage the people that all such obedience is only possible if they first, foremost, and forever abide in Christ in order to receive His life and energy.** Sincere leaders often set the folks up to become "dead branches" and then expect them to bear fruit! Ironically, these "dead branches" may in fact be good "church people." Good "church people" serve on committees, appear overtly pious, faithfully attend worship, participate in Sunday School or Bible study, give tithes and offerings—all "good" deeds for sure, and not without merit. However, when we exhort faithful "doing" out of obedience to Christ, we often set people up to live in fear and guilt because they fail to measure up to the high bars we set. Or, we set them up to falsely and smugly trust in external religiosity, a contemporary pharisaical legalism. A critical question becomes, how can we, as leaders, equip people to become disciples, rather than to be good church people? The solution begins by exhorting people to abide first and allow Christ to fuel and direct the doing.

At this point, I invite you to pause and reflect. **Are you developing into a good "church leader" or into a Serving Leader?** As a member of the People of God, **a leader is nothing if s/he is not disciple first and leader second.** In your mind, what is the difference between a "church person" and a "disciple"? between a "church leader" and a "serving leader"? Reflect.

_____

_____

_____

_____

_____

_____

_____

Have you experienced Christ's baptism and truly been buried with Him in death, dying to self and then rising again in his resurrection life? **Does Christ's presence and power fuel and direct your living and serving as you abide in Him?** Or, are you trapped in a pattern of striving as you attempt to be obedient—"rich" in service and pious practices but poor in life-giving energy? Reflect.

_____

_____

_____

_____

_____

_____

Leaders may desire to be servants; many aspire to be Serving Leaders, but they wind up tired and frustrated, dried up and withered, because they miss the good news that fruitfulness comes from abiding. Or, leaders may become deceived into believing that their production equals true fruitfulness. Just as a branch needs the nutrients of its vine, so do we find our source of strength and energy by abiding in Christ and feasting on His Word (John 15: 3, 7). A servant may be a busy doer, utilizing many personal resources, but a **friend** abides in a committed, intimate, and loving relationship. Remarkably, Jesus invites us to be His friends as we abide in Him (John 15: 12-16).

Just as discipleship cannot be attained by striving, one does not arrive at Serving Leadership by "trying harder." We raise this bar, paradoxically, by relinquishing all of our standards to Christ. **The high standard we set is rooted in yielding to Him. Our standard—our bar—is abandoned. His standard—His bar—is all that matters** and we don't achieve His standard. Christ achieves whatever is worthy, and He does it in and through the yielded life we give Him. This is how we bear much fruit and give all the credit to God, according to Jesus.

Saying it another way, we Raise the Bar, paradoxically, by abandoning all human bars in favor of the exalted bar of Christ's Cross. The Resurrection power that rolled away the stone becomes available to the disciple who abides in the risen Christ. Now a disciple is free to walk with Christ by abiding in Him; now a leader is liberated to lean into Serving Leadership and to Raise the Bar for others by inviting them to embody the baptismal reality of life out of death. Receive Christ's life in all its abundance, today!

The Serving Leader's location—in Christ

I'm sure you've had the experience of navigating your way through a shopping mall or airport and pausing before the map of the facility. Each map posted at a particular location in the venue, displays a large arrow with the words, "You Are Here." That locus on the map serves to orient you and ultimately show you the way to your destination. On the journey of discipleship, each Christian must locate that point of orientation which actually serves as an inner compass for the disciple—You Are Here. What is this critical North Star for the disciple? It is our location in Christ.

To be a Christian is to be in Christ. Sadly, many people walk life's path believing that being a Christian is living in accordance with a set of behavioral norms, or ordering their lives in reaction against "secular" culture. As Dominic Smart points out in his beautiful little book, When We Get it Wrong[21], the term "in Christ" is the avenue for Christian existence presented in the New Testament. The word "Christian" only occurs three times (Acts 11:26; 26:28, 1 Peter 4:16), but the phrase "in Christ" is used no fewer than 115 times. Other relevant passages, such as Colossians 3:1-4 do not use the exact phrase, but refer to the same reality of life in Christ. Spending time in prayer, meditation, and contemplation on these many

---

21 Dominic Smart, When We Get it Wrong: Peter, Christ and our Path through Failure, (Paternoster Lifestyle Publishing, 2001).

Scriptural passages is a life-giving exercise in receiving God's love, grace, and mercy and leads toward owning your identity as a child of God in Christ.

Smart outlines his premise in writing, "We are saved not only by Christ, but in Christ. Not only did he die for us, but we also died with him. Not only did he rise for us, but we also rise in him."[22] Smart's overarching theme becomes Christ's finished work. Not only is our salvation complete in Christ, but so is our discipleship. Because Christ-followers are in Him, Christ's fully lived and completed discipleship is ours. The life I live as a disciple is lived in Christ, therefore I need not achieve discipleship on my own or for myself—Christ has accomplished it for me. Rather than striving to attain something that has already been completed on my behalf, I need only settle into Christ's finished work. My identity in Christ and the fueling of the Holy Spirit inform and fuel my discipleship. The same is true for you. Isn't that beautiful? I think that's what Paul referred to when he wrote, "Not that I have already obtained all this, or have been made perfect, but I press on to take hold of that for which Christ Jesus took hold of me" (Philippians 3:12).

Suppose someone built a house for you, gave you the deed, and invited you to take ownership of it and dwell in it as its permanent resident. You would move right in, grateful for the amazingly gracious gift! It would become your place of residence. You would not work at building your house (that would

---

22 Ibid, 7.

be ridiculous), it's already finished—there is no more work to do; you get to enjoy the benefit of the builder's work. So it is with Christ. Smart observes,

> "Therefore a staggeringly different view of discipleship emerges. It is this: my discipleship (all my repentance, obedience, service, action, praying, you name it), seen as an offering to the Father, is acceptable because I am 'in Christ' who has already 'done' discipleship for me, and done it perfectly... Our walk with Christ has a context: that of being in Christ, in whom all that I have and am, and all that I will be for God, is acceptable because of the perfect Son in whom I have my entire being. All my repentance, my service and my offerings are accepted not because they are good enough for a holy God, nor because God drops his standards. (God cannot drop his standards because they are the reflection of his glory.) They are accepted and pleasing to God because I bring them in and through the Lord Jesus Christ, and can bring them no other way. By the same token, my repentance, service and offerings of time, talents and money are not rejected because they are sub-standard, but rather accepted because I bring them in Christ in whom they are made right... Being a disciple then, is a matter of being in Christ..."[23]

We have asserted, earlier, that being a Serving Leader is predicated on being a disciple; therefore, to use Smart's line of reasoning, **Being a Serving Leader, then, is a matter of being in Christ.**

As Smart rightly points out, we live in an age of pragmatism—

---

23 Ibid, 8-9.

one in which we place a high premium on usefulness, productivity, efficiency, and results. Such pragmatism serves to create
a false view of what is important for a disciple of Jesus. We
run the great danger of putting what we do before who we are,
and approach Christian living (and leadership) apart from the
context of our identity in Christ. We are driven by a Christian
legalism that says, essentially, "I can make myself acceptable to
God by what I do." This attitude is self-realizing, instead of
accepting the realization of Christ in us and us in Him. Smart
critiques this posture as,

> "Works mad, because it knows nothing of the rest that comes
> through faith in Christ. It panders to our activist natures—those
> who are energetic and well-organized can be especially susceptible
> to its poisonous charms. It is alien to grace and mercy. It is of the
> flesh, not the Spirit. It substitutes the word of God for the traditions
> of men… The approach has a rationale which goes something like
> this. As far as my conversion was concerned, that was a matter of
> God's grace… But then, once saved, it's a different matter. Now we
> can, no, we must do those things which can (so we think) ensure
> our continuing acceptability to God. We were initially accepted by
> God on the basis of his love for us, but now, being capable of do-
> ing good, we must maintain our acceptability by keeping the good
> works tally high… we were justified by God's grace through faith in
> Christ, but practically speaking we think and act as if we are sanc-
> tified by pulling ourselves up by our own boot straps."[24]

The good news for leaders is that you can rest! You can rest in

---

24 Ibid, 10-12.

the finished work of Christ even in the midst of your hectic schedule, never-ending to-do lists, and unfinished business. Secondly, overworked leaders can take a day off! (Indeed, you must take days off, and build the rhythm of Sabbath-keeping into your life.) Thirdly, you are free to re-order your life into a holistic reality—one in which all components have been embraced and redeemed by God (I describe this reality through the "Bagel Effect" in the theological foundations section of this chapter). As we look at the witness of Christ's leadership with the disciples, strikingly He gave them very little to do. Their call was to be with Him and learn from Him. As Smart demonstrates, "In the Son, I live my whole life also as a son or daughter of the Father, not as an operative in a deity's factory."[25]

I used to think I had a call to ministry… I have since realized that I have a call to follow. Unlike a call to ministry, the call to follow does not begin with busyness, tasks, or service. The call to follow begins in stillness, with listening, and with a desire for nothing other than God—a response to the Voice of my Creator; ultimately the call to follow is simply to abide in a passionate love-relationship with God, the Holy Trinity. The call to follow begins when I come to the end of myself, and allow Christ to be my all in all. The call to follow is a call to die (Matthew 16:24-26) and also to rise with Him in newness of life. Many a Christian servant becomes worn out, disillusioned, and spent because they have died with Him but haven't risen with Him. Service pours out of the overflow of the love

---

25 Ibid, 14.

relationship. In my call to follow, I become the vessel—the container for God's love. As I live a life of worship, allowing God to fill me daily with His Holy Spirit, then the overflow of His love is expressed through my service. Service stems not from a call to serve, but from a call to love and to follow. My call is not to serve; my call is a call to love and to follow.

Christ's call was to love and to serve (Matthew 20:28). When I attempt to live a call to serve, I wind up doing it in my own strength and limited resources. **When I surrender to a call to follow, then Christ the Savior lives, loves, and serves through me as I become an available vessel for His use.** The Apostle Paul: "To this end [proclaiming the Gospel to the Gentiles] I labor, struggling with all **his** energy, which so powerfully works in me" (Colossians 1:29, emphasis added). In a call to ministry, I tend to struggle in my own energy, becoming weary and worn out; in a call to follow, I have the inexhaustible riches of Christ's glorious grace at work in, through, and beyond me. It is ultimately Christ who builds His church and loves His people. I'm freed to follow Him as He does God's work in the world.

 (Visit www.johnstahlwert.com/TSL for podcast #6 on "Serving Leaders get Results.")

Selecting Leaders

Jennings and Stahl-Wert summarize a key action of a Serving Leader in Raising the Bar; "Serving leaders Raise the Bar of expectation by being highly selective in the choice of team leaders and by establishing high standards of performance.

These actions build a culture of performance throughout the team, business, or community."

Recall that the importance of careful selection in The Serving Leader is first and foremost about making the hard choice of who to pour into based on who can reproduce this powerful Serving Leader approach with others. It isn't about "performance." It's about **building a culture of serving leadership by being highly selective in choosing other leaders who are committed to a way of leading that is rooted in Christ-like servanthood.**

Now let's apply this to the Body of Christ. Think about what it means to be highly selective and to establish high standards of performance in order to Raise the Bar within the Body of Christ. Reflect.

What selection criteria will you look for as you choose team leaders? List:

Name the performance standards you would establish:

_____

_____

_____

_____

_____

_____

_____

_____

Based on the biblical witness, I suggest the following selection criteria as a starting point:

* Candidate is able to articulate a personal definition of "Christ-follower"/"disciple" in keeping with the biblical witness (definition is not theoretical, but rather embodied)

* Candidate is able to describe what it means to be a disciple (identity) and relate specific behaviors (doing) that spring from their identity in Christ

* Candidate walks daily in the clear understanding that s/he is "in Christ" and relies firmly on the power of the Holy Spirit for daily living

* Candidate discerns a unique spiritual gift or gift-mix that s/he brings to the Body of Christ and people in the faith community recognize and affirm these gifts

* Candidate's unique SHAPE [Spiritual gift(s), Heart (passions), Abilities, Personality, and Experience][26] matches the written job description for the leadership position to

_____

26 For more information on SHAPE and SHAPE discovery, see Saddleback Church, www.saddleback.com.

> be filled
*   Candidate senses God's call to the leadership position and people in leadership affirm and confirm that call

Based on the biblical witness, I suggest the following performance standards as a starting point:

*   Leader demonstrates a robust life in Christ characterized by worship, prayer, other spiritual disciplines, generosity, fellowship with other believers, and service
*   Leader lives within a rhythm of Sabbath-keeping
*   Leader embodies an "others-focused" not self-centered posture
*   Leader develops and is accountable to a personal discipleship plan
*   Leader develops and is accountable to a personal/professional growth plan

You will notice that I've said nothing about the leader's specific job or adherence to the roles and responsibilities laid out in a particular job description. The job description and accountability to it is extremely important, and actual performance standards should measure against it. If the leader bears witness to the five key standards outlined above, however, the details of job performance (role and tasks) will fall into place, as long as the individual is well suited for the position. Remember Christ's promise: "If a man remains in me and I in him, he **will** bear much fruit..." (John 15:5b). God is faithful to bring forth fruit from the leader who is first and foremost a disciple of Christ and seeks to abide in Him.

We raise the leadership bar by raising the discipleship bar. Just as we dare not set performance standards for discipleship without helping to ground the disciple firmly in her identity in Christ, we must not establish performance standards for leadership without helping to ground the leader firmly in her discipleship.[27] When organizations like the Church establish performance standards alone, they reduce leadership to an exercise in checking off to-do lists and accomplishing metrics rather than developing people and leading them in Christ's mission of disciple-making. One can excel at the highest levels of leadership and win all kinds of performance awards ("rich" like the young ruler), but live a tragically unfruitful life if unconnected firmly to the Vine who gives life and life abundant. Leaders, raising the bar in this fashion requires a paradigm shift for many, but be encouraged! In the triumphant words of the Apostle Paul, "I can do everything through him [Christ] who gives me strength" (Philippians 4:13).

---

27 To be clear, we are not arguing for the elimination of performance standards in an organization, nor are we renouncing the leader's responsibility to invite people to challenge themselves to stretch, develop, and excel according to their strengths and abilities. Establishing benchmarks, setting goals, and holding team members accountable to reaching those raised bars differentiate vibrant, robust organizations from those that flounder and fail. Scripture bears witness to the pursuit of excellence. One example among many is Paul's exhortation to the Corinthians, "Run in such a way as to get the prize. Everyone who competes in the games goes into strict training... Therefore I do not run like a man running aimlessly." (1Cor. 9:24b-26a). In this apologetic, we simply Raise the Bar of awareness around what we believe is God's heart and directive for fruitful and abundant life, discipleship, and ultimately leadership in Christ.

To serve the many, serve the few

Jesus loved paradox! Christ's teachings constantly turned conventional wisdom on its head, and His behaviors and practices evidenced His zeal for contradicting the status quo. The New Testament writers elaborated on the power of paradox in the Gospel message. For example, Paul writes, "For the foolishness of God is wiser than man's wisdom, and the weakness of God is stronger than man's strength" (1 Corinthians 1:25). Jesus embodied God's wisdom by the manner in which He chose and equipped His disciples—an approach that many might consider foolish in today's high efficiency, mass-market world.

Jesus overturned convention when He selected the Twelve. Standard practice for a rabbi of Jesus' day involved careful selection of only the best of the best among the pool of potential disciples. Only the best and brightest students were chosen for the high honor and privilege of becoming a particular rabbi's disciples. Disciples were by definition, ones who followed a particular rabbi—living life with him, learning from him, gaining knowledge through his wisdom, teaching, and experience. A defined process weeded out the less intelligent students and those of poor estate or ones lacking in motivation. During childhood, boys were identified as having potential to succeed as a rabbi's disciples, and were groomed and developed for such an opportunity.

When Jesus was ready to select His followers—His disciples—He looked not to the best and brightest; he sought out the dropouts! Christ went to the pool of men who hadn't made the cut; He searched for the rejects. Christ's disciples were fishermen, tax collectors, and tradesmen—men who had long since left formal education, and may indeed have never been candidates for it. Paradoxically, Jesus Raised the Bar by rejecting human standards. He saw potential not in worldly means or in external qualities alone, but in the content of men's character and in their God-given potential. In order to release potential in his disciples, and subsequently in others, Christ paradoxically chose **to invest in the few in order to serve the many**.

In his very helpful book, Transforming Discipleship[28], pastor and author Dr. Greg Ogden constructs a model for developing people as disciples of Christ. His model is based on Christ's principles and practices with his twelve disciples. As Ogden describes the attitudes, postures, and practices that characterize disciple-making leaders, he in essence characterizes Serving Leadership. Ogden maintains that Christ's choosing to focus on a few people—the Twelve—was strategic and essential to the ultimate task of multiplying disciples. As he writes about Christ's selection of the particular twelve men, Ogden relates, "My best guess is that Jesus was not so much trying to settle on the right ones as he was praying that they would become the right ones."[29] Christ recognized potential and was keen on cultivating and releasing it. As Ogden observes, Jesus' ultimate goal was to make self-initiating, reproducing, fully devoted followers. In order to best meet this goal, which ultimately was about serving the many, Christ chose to invest in the few.

---

28 Greg Ogden, Transforming Discipleship: Making Disciples a Few at a Time, (Downers Grove, IL: InterVarsity Press), 2003.
29 Ibid, 63.

According to Ogden, Christ's strategy involved two main thrusts, internalization and multiplication.[30] Christ's life and mission needed to be internalized in the lives of His followers. The only way to authentically and effectively accomplish this objective was through cultivating intimate relationships. People-development is fundamentally a relational process. It is not achieved by cranking out disciples on an assembly line or through programs and formal processes. It is startling to note that Jesus left no memoirs and no personal training manual—nothing penned by His own hand. He appeared to rely on two means to carry His life and mission forward: the Holy Spirit and the Twelve.[31] Jesus intentionally built relationships and invested in a small inner circle in order to accomplish the larger work of His Father's Kingdom.

One might inquire, "given Jesus' focus on the Twelve, does that mean He was unconcerned about the masses?" On the contrary, Jesus' vision was for the masses as He maintained His focus on the few. Ogden captures the wisdom well, "The irony is that in our attempt to reach the masses through mass means we have failed to train people the masses could emulate. We often perpetuate superficiality by casting a wider net, without the commensurate depth. Jesus multiplied his life in the Twelve so that there would be more of himself to go around... By investing in a few, Jesus intended to transfer his life to others, so that they would be about this business of extending his redemptive life to the multitudes."[32]

---

30 Ibid, 65.
31 Ibid, 68.
32 Ibid, 69, 70.

Serving Leaders share Jesus' heart for the masses and ultimately desire that all people within their sphere of influence would be developed to their full potential. Savvy Serving Leaders do well to adopt Jesus' two-pronged approach of internalization and multiplication.

As you think about internalization, what are some steps you can take to build authentic relationships with a few key people? Who are the few that you feel called to invest in?

_____

_____

_____

_____

_____

_____

_____

As you invest in the few, relationally, what are the main components of your vision that you wish to impart to them? What are the core values, beliefs, and convictions that you hold most closely that you feel led to share?

_____

_____

_____

_____

_____

_____

_____

Think of a "ripple effect." Just as a pebble thrown into a pool creates a ripple of waves that multiply as they spread, so do relationships that multiply intentionally. As you invest in a few key leaders, invite them to pray about who their "few" will be. Over time, equip your inner circle to develop their own inner circle and train them to invest in these new groups. If you're a leader in a congregation, you may want to think about this "ripple effect" in terms of your process for disciple-making. Regardless of the organization you serve, the principle (and paradox) of serving the many by investing in the few becomes the strategic avenue for advancing vision, instilling ownership, working strategically toward objectives, and growing the organization by growing its people.

Finally, as we think biblically about Raising the Bar in the context of Serving Leadership, we can relate it to the doctrine of sanctification, or "going on to perfection" as theologian John Wesley described it. Many theories on this doctrine prevail, but I liken it to spiritual formation, or the maturing process of being formed in Christ through the power of the indwelling Holy Spirit. As we Raise the Bar for the people we serve, it is a privilege to call them higher and invite them onward in their journey in Christ. As a Serving Leader, pray for your people as Paul did, "We are glad whenever we are weak but you are strong; and our prayer is for your perfection" (2 Corinthians 13:9). And exhort the people as Paul did, "Aim for perfection, listen to my appeal, be of one mind, live in peace. And the God of love and peace will be with you" (2 Corinthians 13:11b).

✝ Theological Foundations

In our busy, performance-driven culture, many leaders find it difficult to abide; to cease striving and accomplishing long enough to discover what it means to reside in Christ and to find identity there; and then to allow their "in Christ-ness" to inform and guide their performance. A different qualitative metric is needed; one that can be considered using the metaphor of a common breakfast food.

The Bagel Effect

Sociologist, musician, and corporate executive Paul Hoffert, in his book The Bagel Effect,[33] describes a contemporary world where society, culture, and economy are moving from a slow, centralized, "cream puff" configuration to a swift paced, distributed "bagel" formation where the real action occurs at the rim and not at the controlling core. He describes the pendulum swing from security, safety, order, and control (the "cream puff"); to freedom, risk, chaos, choice, individual rights (the "bagel"), which he maintains is concurrent with the digital revolution. Hoffert asserts that when a society's strong, inner locus of control collapses, power struggles, caucuses, and centers of control form at the margins, and consequently societal energy distributes to the outer margins.

33 Paul Hoffert, The Bagel Effect: A Compass to Navigate the Wired World, (McGraw-Hill Ryerson Press), 1998.

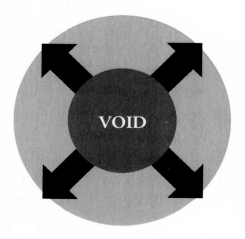

Hoffert's Bagel Effect can be extrapolated from society to the Church. If a church loses the centrality of Christ at her core, all power and energy pushes to the margins because the core becomes void. This subtle shift can occur when a church and her leaders neglect prayer, allow human strategy and thinking to usurp God's wisdom, denigrate scriptural primacy, etc. As a result, special interest groups, strong personalities, programs, church business models, charismatic leaders begin to seek power and control. When the church syncretizes with the culture and loses her heart, the church becomes institutionalized, and exists to support the institution rather than the mission of Christ.

The church transitions from Man (Body of Christ), to Movement, to Method, to Machine, to Monument.[34]

34 Dr. Chris Hardy and Dr. Elizabeth Wourms applied the theory of the "Bagel Effect" to Christian leaders after hearing a lecture by the Rev. Dr. Ed Zeiders at a Doctor of Ministry Intensive session at United Theological

When this shift occurs, the church loses the core of its being. It doesn't just lose its focus; it loses its heart—its heart for existence.

When Christ remains at the core, using the Bagel Effect, all energy, focus, power, and control remain with Him. All aspects of Body life orient toward the core of the Church—Christ, and indeed find their identity, order, and direction from Christ their Core. Such a church bears witness to the biblical reality, "'For in him we live and move and have our being...'" (Acts 17:28).

The Bagel Effect applies to Christian leaders, as well, and this principle directly impacts Raising the Bar for our team members and the people in our congregations and organizations.

If you are like most people, you tend to think of your life in segmented components. You have your family life, your work life, your ministry life, and if you are fortunate, your personal life. When you think of "balance" in your life, you probably think about trying to give each separate component equal attention, or to make them roughly equal in terms of your time, energy, and focus. You likely Raise the Bar for yourself continuously, desiring to be a better parent, a better self, a more effective leader. Naming some of these typical elements of your life, you might arrange them something like the graph-

---

Seminary in January, 2007. Dr. Zeiders argued convincingly for the adoption of Hoffert's Bagel Effect as an explanation for the identity struggles facing many Western churches. Dr. Zeiders referenced Dr. Vance Havner in describing the transition from "man" to "monument."

ic below in an attempt to visualize "balance" and hold all the components together. They gather at the outer margins of your "bagel."

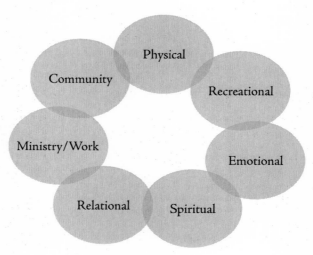

The problem with segmented thinking, striving for balance for the whole, and success in the parts is that you, the individual, bear the burden of having to achieve or attain the desired outcome. Laboring in your own strength, you often become weary, discouraged, and despairing in trying to attain the elusive holy grail of peace, happiness, contentment, and success. Patterns of behavior that lead to a life "out of balance" are engrained. Each "component" of your life becomes just one more thing vying for energy, attention, priority, and accomplishment. The center is void, and so power struggles ensue at the margins.

The Bible teaches that shalom is a holistic reality—indeed, life is a holistic reality. The biblical Hebrews viewed individuals as whole beings. It was the ancient Greek philosophers who introduced our Western understanding of dualism—of the divided nature of a human being into "spirit" and "flesh" or "body" and "soul." The unbiblical concept of a divided self developed into an even more fractured understanding that life itself was divided into compartments, or silos—work, family, ministry, recreation, personal care—with fairly rigid boundaries around each one.

God views you as a whole person. God sees your life as a whole entity. Your life is one wonderful conglomeration of all the attributes, relationships, and situations that comprise your reality. **As a Christian servant, it is vital that you realize and own the fact that all of life is ministry, and all of ministry is life!** Your family is not separate from your ministry—your family is your ministry. Your ministry must take place in your home before it goes anywhere else. Your job is not separate from your ministry; your job is your ministry. Your personal life is not separate from your ministry—enjoying hobbies, recreation, eating well, getting adequate rest—all are ministry. Fundamentally, ministry, or service, is a response to God, flowing out of one's relationship with God through Christ. **Your identity is Follower of Jesus, not Pastor or Christian Leader.** Do not allow ministry to be trivialized and reduced to the job for which you earn a paycheck, or the functions you perform professionally. Do not allow ministry-as-job to become a hungry beast that consumes all the other aspects of your life.

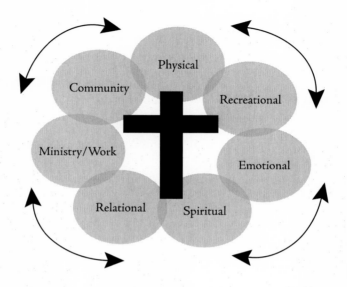

Picture your life as a "cream puff" with Christ filling the void in the center. Christ at your life's center paints a holistic and liberating picture. This concept completely deconstructs the "life balance" or "bagel" model with the spheres all competing at life's margins.

With Christ at the center of your life, you are free to cease striving for balance in the whole and success in the spheres and thus to allow Him to bring order, direction, and shalom to your life. The circles might wind up being different sizes, but when each area of a holistic life are yielded to the Holy Spirit's control, then true shalom is possible. Ultimately, then, authentic Serving Leadership becomes possible.

Consider the following Scripture.

When the day of Pentecost came, they were all together in one place. Suddenly a sound like the blowing of a violent wind came from heaven and filled the whole house where they were sitting. They saw what seemed to be tongues of fire that separated and <u>came to rest</u> on each of them. All of them were filled with the Holy Spirit (Acts 2:1-4a) [emphasis added].

The term in Greek that is translated "came to rest" is a word that literally means a person of great authority coming to sit in a place of great authority. It is a term reserved for kings, or ruling authorities, reigning from a throne. When you allow Christ to occupy the center of your "bagel," you give Him freedom to **reign from the throne of your life**. This is what we mean when we say "Jesus is Lord." When you allow a void to develop in the center of your "bagel," whether by your own striving, hectic schedule, or spiritual neglect, you have in effect pushed Christ off the throne of your life. Christ reigns eternally from His throne in heaven, at the right hand of the Father, and nothing can shake that position. Believers can and do knock Christ off the throne of their own lives, however, as we allow deception to creep in, either through self, the world, or Satan.

So what does the Bagel Effect have to do with Raising the Bar? Through the indwelling Holy Spirit, God will help you to move from balance toward shalom; and from "success" to significance and sustainability. With Christ at the center of your "bagel," sustainable leadership is not only possible, it is contagious. More importantly, sustainable, abundant life is evident.

Paradoxically, leaders Raise the Bar for others as they set the bar to the basics of the Christian faith. As Christians, we are nothing if we are not **Christ-centered**. A challenging reach-up becomes a challenging reach-back—inviting others to rein in the components of a life fragmented at the margins and to collect it all as a life centered, complete, and whole in Christ. When Christ reigns from the throne of your life, when Christ reigns from the throne of your team members' lives, then He is able to accomplish great things in, through, among, and beyond you for the sake of His glory.

"To this end I labor, struggling with all his energy, which so powerfully works in me" (Colossians 1:29).

Pause and pray... Lord Jesus, I acknowledge You as the Sovereign Lord of my life. Just a You filled the believers at Pentecost and caused Your Holy Spirit to reign from the throne of their lives, please come and fill me with Your Fullness. Lord Jesus, come and reign from the throne of my life. Amen.

Raising the Bar through Encouragement

If a primary function of the Serving Leader is to extend "challenging reach-ups" to team members, leaders, and volunteers in the organization, through what practical means does a leader adopt this competency? **Developing a leadership posture of authentic care and supportive guidance becomes primary.** In his first letter to the Thessalonians, Paul writes tenderly, employing the metaphor of parent to describe his leadership among the people. Paul writes, "but we were gentle among you, like a mother caring for her little children. We loved you so much that we were delighted to share with you not only the gospel of God but our lives as well, because you had become so dear to us... For you know that we dealt with each of you as a father deals with his own children, encouraging, comforting and urging you to live lives worthy of God, who calls you into his kingdom and glory" (1 Thessalonians 2: 7-8, 11-12). This Scripture paints an extraordinary picture of Serving Leadership. In this passage we see Paul, the leader, passionately loving the people—loving them enough to share his life in addition to sharing the Gospel. Often in ministry, we hear the warning: "Don't get too close to the people you serve," or "you should never become friends with people in your congregation." That posture seems tragic in light of this biblical witness! Paul seems to invite leaders to a level of intimacy, authenticity, and transparency with the people with whom they are called into community. Paul's leadership was predicated on the internalization that Ogden advocates (see Biblical Foundations section).

Paul, the leader, is gentle, loving, and caring; he encourages, comforts, and urges the people to live lives worthy of the God they serve. One of Paul's favorite verbs, found frequently in his letters, is parakaleo. Literally, parakaleo means "to call alongside." In Scripture, parakaleo is translated variously as "ask, beg, plead, urge, call, exhort, invite, appeal to, answer kindly, comfort, encourage,"—all nuances that help us understand this vital verb that is foundational to Serving Leadership—consider these examples from Scripture:

"Therefore encourage one another and build each other up, just

as in fact you are doing" (1 Thessalonians 5:11).

"But encourage one another daily, as long as it is called Today, so that none of you may be hardened by sin's deceitfulness" (Hebrews 3:13).

"Praise be to... the God of all comfort, who comforts us in all our troubles, so that we can comfort those in any trouble with the comfort we ourselves have received from God" (2 Corinthians 1:3-4).

"I urge you, brothers [and sisters], by our Lord Jesus Christ and by the love of the Spirit, to join me in my struggle by praying to God for me."[NIV] or "to strive together with me in your prayers to God for me." [NASB] (Romans 15:30).

The title Paraklete, which is often used for the Holy Spirit, derives from the root of this word parakaleo. Used in this way, a Paraklete is a legal advisor, counselor, advocate, or helper. Serving Leaders embody these qualities of counselor, advocate, and helper as they lovingly serve and equip the people in their spheres of influence.

As leaders live into this call to love, encourage, and offer supportive guidance, they simply walk alongside (parakaleo) the people with whom they lead and serve. **In the role of Serving Leader, an individual seeks to engage individual and team potential, shaping it into achievable plans and releasing it into action.** The leader's role is to make it easier for the team to do its work. By providing non-directive leadership, the

Serving Leader helps the team arrive at decisions collabora-
tively. **The leader's role is one of assistance and guidance,
not control. Serving Leadership is evidenced when the team
is concerned not only with a decision that is made, but also
with the way the decision is made.** The leader is an individual
whose recognized job is to help manage a process of information exchange. Thus, their role is to help with HOW the dis-
cussion/process is proceeding and has **responsibility in addressing the journey, rather than just the destination.**

The highlighted words and phrases in the preceding paragraph
emphasize the caring and supportive posture of the Serving
Leader. These leaders are primarily motivated by love, compassion, and concern for the people; and secondarily motivated by goals, objectives, outcomes, and the bottom line. Developing people and releasing their potential, thus catalyzing
the creation of high-performing teams made up of fully alive
people trumps a focus on tasks and action every time. The Key
Behaviors and Practices section at the end of this chapter lifts
up some postures and behaviors that Serving Leaders exhibit
as they live into this biblical attitude of encouragement.

The Excellence of Our Work[35]

As we Raise the Bar, both for self as leader, and for the people
we serve, we do well to remember that God invites us to standards of excellence in our work. Indeed, God inherently raised
the bar for us as human beings when our Creator formed us
in His image. God is infinitely creative; as humans created in

---

35 The genesis for this section of the chapter is a fruitful and evocative conversation that took place between John Stahl-Wert and Merle Herr.

God's image, we are blessed with vast creative potential and the capacity to perform good work. That we might be creative and accomplished is part of God's perfect plan. Consider the account from Genesis.

"So God created man in his own image, in the image of God he created him; male and female he created them. God blessed them and said to them, 'Be fruitful and increase in number; fill the earth and subdue it. Rule over the fish of the sea and the birds of the air and over every living creature that moves on the ground.' Then God said, 'I give you every seed-bearing plant on the face of the whole earth and every tree that has fruit with seed in it. They will be yours for food'... God saw all that he had made, and it was very good... The LORD God took the man and put him in the Garden of Eden to work it and take care of it" (Genesis 1:27-31a; 2:15).

In the beginning of creation, before the introduction of sin, Adam and Eve lived in freedom within the perfect plan of God. God desired that they work and work well—to be fruitful and multiply, to tend the flora and fauna of the Garden. As God surveyed the creation and His plan for the people, God declared it all **very good**. (Notice that at this point in the account, the created order is deemed **very** good; earlier in the narrative, the elements of creation are declared good.) I can imagine God walking with Adam in the Garden during the cool of the day, enjoying intimate fellowship with His beloved, and delighting in Adam's fruitfulness—in his work. Picture Adam running to God and exclaiming, "Come and see what I've done today!" As Adam accomplished the work set before him by the Creator, God surely affirmed him and celebrated his efforts.

As Paul recognized, "We are God's workmanship, created in Christ Jesus to do good works, which God prepared in advance for us to do" (Ephesians 2:10). Just as God created Adam for good work, God created you and me for good work as part of His eternal plan of creation and co-creation. Indeed, our work is worship. Paul urges, "offer your bodies as living sacrifices, holy and pleasing to God—this is your spiritual act of worship" (Romans 12:1). As we offer our whole selves to God, including the work of our hands, God receives our gift as worship. God invites us to press toward high standards of justice, beauty, excellence, and shalom as we engage in fruitful endeavors. Our work brings glory to God as we offer it in worship, as we are drawn up into God's purposes through the indwelling Christ and the Holy Spirit who fuels and informs our work. Godly work is sacramental; God receives our best work and infuses it with His grace in order to make it acceptable in His sight and a blessing to others. Such work is not our own; such work is God's as He uses it to advance His reign. If our work is excellent, then the Kingdom advances. The work, however, is not about performance, it is about love; the work is not for our glory, it is about God's glory. In the mystery of God's purposes, our work is somehow eternal as God pulls it up into His presence.

And so, as we Raise the Bar, for ourselves and others, we do so within the wonder of God's plan for fruitfulness and excellence. As Serving Leaders we live in the tension that God invites us higher (the raised bar of excellence) and yet invites us "lower" to a posture of humility clothed in Christ's sufferings and His resurrection life.

Ultimately, Raising the Bar is all about people-development and assisting folks to realize their full potential in Christ. This practice is both a responsibility and a high privilege for all Serving Leaders.

⚷ Key Behaviors and Practices

Following are some key behaviors and practices that you might consider adopting as you seek to more fully embody the Serving Leader Powerful Action, Raise the Bar. After reading this chapter, you may be thinking, **HOW** do I become a leader who is able to successfully Raise the Bar? We hope you find some helpful suggestions here. You may also find it beneficial to discuss your key learnings and "ah-ha's" with a trusted mentor or coach. S/he can assist you in making key behavior changes, encourage you to take risks, and challenge you to stretch outside your comfort zone.

For reflection, contemplation, perhaps journaling:

* Prayerfully, and through searching Scripture, articulate your personal definition of "disciple." What does it mean to be a disciple, or Christ-follower? What types of practices, attitudes, and postures flow out of that being, and hence what does a disciple do?
* How can YOU more fully become a disciple of Christ

and how can you equip others to grow in their discipleship in Christ?

* Over 115 New Testament Scriptures speak to the reality of your life **in Christ**. What does that biblical reality mean to you, personally? How does your location—your dwelling place—in Christ influence your sense of identity, your behavior, your attitudes, your practices, your ministry, your leadership?

Key Practices:
Ensure trust on your team and throughout the organization.

<u>Key Actions:</u>
* Follow through on what you say (integrity)
* Value and receive all input from people on your team
* Affirm people always (even when you disagree)
* Challenge the process not the person during debate or decision-making
* Establish ground rules and group norms (covenant) and stick with them (encourage healthy conflict engagement)
* Help people get acquainted and build relationships on the team
* Be vulnerable and transparent as a leader
* Engage and manage conflict in a healthy manner
* Silence is acquiescence—speak openly, directly, and honestly
* Engage in "unfiltered ideological debate" on issues and discussion points
    ▪ Take a time out to affirm people if discussion becomes heated

- Act as referee when needed
- Protect
- Redirect

Extend ownership of vision, strategy, and responsibilities to your team members

Key Actions:
* Ask people what pieces of the work they feel led to assume
* Assign responsibilities, clear next-steps, and accountability structures
* Release people to carry out responsibilities according to gifts and passion
  - Assist people in identifying their gifts and passion
  - Invite them to participate with you in a particular service or ministry that fits their gifts and passion. Following is a helpful progression:
    - I (the leader) do; You (the person) watch
    - I do; You help
    - You do: I help
    - You do; I watch[36]
  - Share leadership—let someone else facilitate meetings and project management; make presentations
  - Share control
  - Share accountability for outcomes (because control is shared, so is accountability for outcomes—team members are jointly responsible for decisions and subsequent action (or inaction)

36 Ogden, 2003, Chapter 4. Ogden provides a helpful model of empowerment according to Jesus' life and practice as evidenced in the Scriptures.

* Empower people

Key Actions:
* Affirm and value people for who they are; communicate your affirmation verbally and in writing
  ▪ Recognize people for what they do—privately (1:1) and publicly
  ▪ Celebrate team successes
  ▪ Ensure clear communication—check for understanding
  ▪ Give people the tools they need to be successful and effective
  ▪ Ask: "what do you need in order to be your best self?"
  ▪ Resist micromanagement
  ▪ Allow differing approaches to a specific challenge/task
  ▪ Provide means for people to become more self-aware by encouraging self-reflection, providing regular feedback, and utilizing assessment instruments
  ▪ Assist people to develop personal and ministry action plans. ("being" first; ministry effectiveness second)
  ▪ Provide opportunities for training and re-tooling
  ▪ Provide opportunities for people to experience times of personal Sabbath
  ▪ Encourage spiritual growth and discipleship

 (Visit www.johnstahlwert.com/TSL for podcast #7 on "Raise the Bar.")

🗣 A Real-Life Story

By Rick Shonkwiler, senior minister at White Oak Christian Church in Cincinnati, Ohio

I knew I was in trouble when I looked at the "to do" list for our upcoming men's conference. Much of the leadership that was required needed to be men who were growing in their relationship to Christ. And, I did not have that big of a list.

While I recruited and empowered men to serve in that conference, I knew I could not continue developing a ministry without developing the people to oversee and accomplish the ministry. At about the same time, I heard someone say, "One transformed man transforms many things!" I had to Raise the Bar and challenge men to grow into leadership.

From that conference, I recruited 10 men to begin a weekly small group. We initially studied materials related to the conference, but soon moved on to other material. We landed on four books that would lead us through: handling temptation, building friendships with other men, loving our wives (for those who were married), and leading our family. As we moved through these books, I challenged individual men to lead the group discussion. This required extra reading and preparation. As a result, I was able to see and evaluate the growth in each man. I could make suggestions and pray specifically for each one.

After a year of study, I challenged the group to expand, by starting two new groups. I continued to lead the original group, which grew back to 10 men, while the two new groups began meeting (with two new leaders for each group). This allowed me to evaluate the new leaders, giving practical insight and training to specific to the groups.

During the second year, we decided to do another men's conference to accomplish many of the goals we had set for challenging, incorporating and encouraging men because of the ownership taken by those in charge. This time, the leaders of the various teams came from the existing groups. Communication and performance of tasks were greatly enhanced because of the relationships built with the men. I also recruited two co-leaders to work directly with me. "Bill" and "Sam" each took a significant part of the conference planning team as direct oversight. They each had budget responsibilities and team building responsibilities. Because the conference was for the church community at large, several men took responsibility to contact churches about the event.

I provided direction to the team and they, in turn, communicated to the population in general. New groups were started and led by men who had been trained in the initial groups.

When we returned, there seemed to be little horsepower for change. I had expectation of a strong ministry, with leadership coming from these two leaders. After returning, I realized that each was in the midst of a personal, work related struggle, and while personally committed to the ministry, each did not have the leadership qualities to bring others along. I had not taken that into consideration as I called for greater commitment.

After evaluating the situation, it was apparent that I needed to select leaders based around how they did at attracting others to the mission. That meant I needed to pour more effort into "Jim" and "Fred." Jim had been a part of my group, had led occasionally, and had shown great promise as he spoke with other men. Fred was a good "idea" man, whom I wanted to challenge to grow bolder in implementing his ideas.

After much prayer and conversation with others (a step I had not fully vetted before), I asked Jim and Fred to go with me to the leadership conference. They accepted and off we went. This time the outcome was different. Each came back ready to lean into the ministry.

By this time, another two years had passed and our ministry was ready for another men's conference. This time Jim and Fred began leading from the initial planning stages. My role shifted to serve as an adviser as they took the responsibility for recruiting and training leaders, setting calendars/deadlines, and communicating with the speaker and his organization. They also worked with our church administrative staff to cover details for the event.

From that event, several new groups were started. This was one of our big goals. We also had an expectation that men from the ministry would begin to participate in other ministries in our church such as outreach/evangelism, benevolence, children and youth ministries, and pastoral care. This began to happen under Jim's leadership.

What made the difference? Raising the Bar includes deliberate and careful selection of leaders. Developing a pool from which to draw is important. That is why we developed the curriculum and groups that met over a two-year period. From those groups we could select leaders that we had seen "in action."

Why did the first two leaders not hit the mark? I was still in the process of developing our core values of leadership, one of which was the ability to draw others into the ministry. The second was the ability to replicate oneself, to confidently "give away" parts of the ministry. I was hasty in selecting the "first available" instead of waiting for the development of leaders. While each of the first two men was willing, I had not yet established their ability to draw and lead others.

In Jim and Fred I had two men with complimentary skills, who were growing as followers of Jesus. Jim had been an Air Force officer and Fred had his own business. As they grew in faith, I could see Jesus transforming them into what He wanted. They also brought to the table an understanding of goal setting and accomplishment that led to high standards of performance.

Less than a year after this training and leadership development cycle was completed, I accepted a call to a new ministry. This team has continued to lead the ministry in high performance without a direct report on staff at that church. They had demonstrated trustworthiness and competence to the level that the church entrusted the continuation and growth of ministry to their leadership. They had learned to coordinate with other ministry teams, document goals and accomplishments for the church leadership to evaluate, and continue to recruit and train leaders based on the system they had in place.

Closing Thought and Questions for Reflection

Of all the Five Actions of the Serving Leader, Raising the Bar has the greatest potential for being misunderstood and misapplied. The leader can very easily become "the enemy" if s/he simply raises standards of performance for others without submitting all leadership to the same standards/core values. Jesus never asked His disciples to do something He wasn't willing to do first out of love for the Father and for them. A Serving Leader does the same.

But Jesus was not a soft leader, just cheering His disciples on. There were times He had to lovingly but strongly confront them and call them back to God's plans and standards. He never lowered the bar of discipleship for anyone. But with high truth and high grace, He enabled them to become all God wanted them to be.

* What motivates you to want to do your best at your job?
* What criteria do you use to evaluate the work of people who report to you?
* How is "performance" to be understood in regards to salvation? In regards to work/ministry?

Blaze the Trail

You then, my son, be strong in the grace that is in Christ Jesus. And the things you have heard me say in the presence of many witnesses entrust to reliable men who will also be qualified to teach others.

(2 Timothy 2:1-2)

Definition: Serving leaders Blaze the Trail by teaching Serving Leader principles and practices and by removing obstacles to performance. These actions multiply the Serving Leader's impact by educating and activating tier after tier of leadership.

Paradoxes: To protect your value, you must give it all away. Your biggest obstacle is the one that hinders someone else.

"Where there is no vision, the people perish…"
Proverbs 29:18a [KJV]

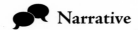

Narrative

The pastoral search committee of Riverside Community Church was having its regular evening meeting in the church's board room. They had had been at this work for four months and were still having a hard time deciding what kind of senior pastor the church needed.

"I'm telling you, we need a strong visionary leader who is an excellent preacher and attracts people," declared Tom. "He needs to have a charismatic personality that demonstrates he's in charge. He needs to get this church in shape and the staff in line. I've had it with the soft leadership we have had here."

Eileen countered, "Yes, we need a good leader and communicator, but if we are depending on the pastor to be the main way to attract people, I think we are heading down the wrong path. Remember what happened at First Church across town—Their new pastor got so far out front of the people that he looked like the enemy. He sure didn't last long."

Charlotte jumped in, "I think people here want a pastor who cares for them and takes things slowly and cautiously. Ministry is about relationships, right? As far as I'm concerned, we have had too many changes here over the years and we don't want to make any more waves."

Just then, there was a knock at the door. Sean Miller, the Director of Youth, poked his head in and said, "Sorry to interrupt you but I just wanted to let you know that I am leaving. I'm going to lock you in, OK?"

"Yeah, that's fine," responded Charles. And then, in a flash of insight, he continued, "Sean, you have been on staff here for three years. What would you like to see in a new senior pastor?"

Sean stepped into the room and saw all eyes were on him. "You want me to be honest?"

"Yes, completely honest."

Sean took a deep breath and said slowly, "I think I can speak for the whole ministry staff. We want someone who values us and invests in us, professionally as well as personally…Someone who doesn't bark orders but rather teaches us how to be better ministry leaders… Someone who listens to our ministry ideas and frustrations and helps remove those frustrations… Someone who "goes to bat for us" and doesn't blame us when things don't go right… Someone who leads us by coming alongside us and helps us become a team, not just a church staff."

Sean paused and then added awkwardly, "I guess you can tell what's been simmering inside me, and all the staff, for some time."

The room was silent.

Sean bit his lip and said, "I think I said too much. I'm sorry…"

"No Sean," replied Charles. "I think you just helped us more than you can imagine."

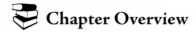 ## Chapter Overview

As the Nike marketing tagline says, "Just do it!" When we think about blazing a trail for the people with whom we're in community, our spirit soars! Simply writing the words makes us want to abandon the computer and dash out into new horizons with a sense of passionate purpose and self-abandonment. This chapter could end here—just do it! Blaze that trail! Such action, however, would be hopelessly idealistic and not a little irrational.

On the leadership spectrum, we find people who eagerly chase dreams and pursue vision, sometimes without plotting a thoughtful course; on the other end of the gamut reside people who tend to resist trail-blazing, whether out of fear, lack of vision, or simply a personality given to deliberate conservatism. Everywhere in between those two poles, gifted leaders struggle to strike a balance between impulsivity and inaction, navigating wisely the path set before them. Serving Leaders make the most of the journey. Along the way, Serving Leaders constantly teach Serving Leadership principles and practices and remove obstacles for others so that they might be unencumbered participants in the mission. **The dual practices of teaching and obstacle-removing become the Serving Leader's primary tool—the machete used to clear the path and Blaze the Trail** so that the people need not fight their way through a dense and tangled trail.

The reflections that follow will guide us all toward pursuing vision with greater courage, resolution, and purpose, always with the greater end in mind, namely blazing the trail by releasing the people to lead the way.

 Biblical Foundations

As trail-blazers, leaders often fix their eyes on the destination and vigorously embark on the quest, looking neither to the right nor to the left. In their zeal, such pioneers often set out at lightning speed, hurtling down the road with only the end in mind. Other leaders, fearful of the journey, begin tentatively, confident of the vision but focused on the dangers, both real and perceived. Both types of leaders may inadvertently hold others back by frustrating and disempowering them. **Serving Leaders retain healthy focus and perspective on both the destination and the journey itself.** Secure in the vision and goal, they remain equally confident that the way to accomplish the mission is to invest in the people who are along for the ride. A familiar adage proclaims the road to ruin is paved with good intentions. Serving Leaders know the road to success is paved with good **investments.** Serving Leaders blaze that trail by investing in people so that collectively everyone achieves the mission together.

Teach and Train
Christ Jesus himself modeled trail-blazing through investment: teaching his followers and removing obstacles to their success. Jesus received knowledge, wisdom, and truth from God the Father and as the ultimate Teacher passed along what He received to His disciples. John records Jesus' assertion,

"I tell you the truth, the Son can do nothing by himself; he can do only what he sees his Father doing, because whatever the Father does the Son also does. For the Father loves the Son and shows him all he does. Yes, to your amazement he will show him even greater things than these. For just as the Father raises the dead and gives them life, even so the Son gives life to whom he is pleased to give it" (John 5:19-21).

Jesus receives life-giving revelation from the Father, imparts it to His followers, and invites them to pass it on. As Serving Leaders, first and foremost as Jesus' disciples, we are both privileged and obligated to share what we have received. Jesus has given you good gifts (including leadership) for your edification and transformation; with the gift comes the commission to invest it in others for their good and ultimately for the advancement of Christ's Kingdom. Later, John adds these words from Christ, "I tell you the truth, anyone who has faith in me will do what I have been doing. He will do even greater things than these, because I am going to the Father" (John 14:12). As people of faith, we are compelled to take up the life of Christ, to do what He did. Serving Leaders are keenly aware of this charge and make every effort to live into it. Christ promises that as we embody His practices, His resurrection power will enable us to do "even greater things." Primary among His practices are teaching and removing obstacles to success. God wisely provides a life-giving channel for growth and development: God teaches and empowers Christ; Christ teaches and empowers leaders; leaders teach and equip people.

Jesus invested enormous amounts of time and energy building relationships, teaching, training, mentoring, and guiding His disciples. These twelve people comprised Jesus' leadership team. He strategically poured into them so that they would grow to greater maturity and readiness to become leaders prepared to pour into others. Jesus developed an apprenticeship for his inner circle. According to the Scriptures, He spent months teaching the disciples—both verbally and through experience as they intimately shared life together—in order to prepare them to be released into the ministry on their own. Prior to sending them out, Jesus provided additional instruction and removed potential obstacles. The Scripture tells us, "He called his twelve disciples to him and gave them authority [removed obstacles] to drive out evil spirits and to heal every disease and sickness... These twelve Jesus sent out with the following instructions..." (Matthew 10:1-5, insertion mine). The thirty-seven verses that follow record the lengthy instruction, which preceded the disciples' dispatch on their mission. Take a moment and read through that passage, noting the various ways in which Christ taught his apprentices and removed obstacles prior to sending them out. Serving Leaders model Christ's process of teaching and proactively removing obstacles.

The Apostle Paul carried Christ's torch and waved the banner of teaching and equipping. As one of Paul's mentees, Timothy received the wisdom, instruction, and experience entrusted to Paul. Teaching and removing obstacles resided at the heart of their relationship. Paul exhorted Timothy,

"So, my son, throw yourself into this work for Christ. *Pass on what you heard from me*—*the whole congregation saying Amen!*—*to reliable leaders who are competent to teach others. When the going gets rough, take it on the chin with the rest of us, the way Jesus did. A soldier on duty doesn't get caught up in making deals at the marketplace. He concentrates on carrying out orders. An athlete who refuses to play by the rules will never get anywhere. It's the diligent farmer who gets the produce. Think it over. God will make it all plain"* [The MSG] (2 Timothy 1-7, emphasis added).

Paul followed the example of Christ as He invested in key leaders, teaching, training, modeling, and releasing them to carry on the mission of the Gospel. As a recipient of godly teaching, training, and instruction, you have a responsibility to pass on what you have received to others **for the expressed purpose that they might be equipped to pass it on.** Too often teaching is imparted to passive recipients who sit on what they have received. Serving Leaders are never content to merely teach; such leaders celebrate a true investment that pays dividends when the recipients multiply the reward in others.

Reflect. When was the last time that you, as leader, provided specific instruction for your team or inner circle in order to equip them for a particular function or mission?

If you do not regularly provide teaching and training for your team, staff, or key leaders—why not?

_____

_____

_____

What would it look like for you to begin an apprenticeship with an emerging leader or group of key leaders in your sphere of influence?

_____

_____

_____

Create an action step for yourself to provide a specific investment in your team, staff, or key leaders sometime in the next month.

_____

_____

_____

Paul knew the value of teaching and training, both for himself, personally, and for the people he served. Employing the metaphor of a runner, Paul writes,

> "Do you not know that in a race all the runners run, but only one gets the prize? Run in such a way as to get the prize. Everyone who competes in the games goes into strict training. They

do it to get a crown that will not last; but we do it to get a crown that will last forever. Therefore I do not run like a man running aimlessly; I do not fight like a man beating the air. No, I beat my body and make it my slave so that after I have preached to others, I myself will not be disqualified for the prize" (1 Corinthians 9:24-27).

An athlete would never dream of stepping onto the playing field or racetrack without training. As leaders, we should never put people in the uncomfortable position of being ill-prepared for the "playing field" of ministry. Paul states the obvious: everyone who competes in the games goes into strict training. Tragically, in many organizations people (volunteers and paid staff alike) are tossed into the waters of work and left to either sink or swim with very little preparation or ongoing training. Emerging leaders bring God-given potential for fruitfulness and success; they may or may not possess the ability (skills, knowledge, experience) for fruitfulness and success. Lack of training, mentoring, and coaching presents a significant obstacle to success for both volunteers and paid staff in an organization. Serving Leaders ensure that the biblical example of teaching and training is carried out in their organizations.

 (Visit www.johnstahlwert.com/TSL for podcast #8 on "Blaze the Trail.")

Remove Obstacles

As Jesus taught His followers, He remained on the lookout for "teachable moments." These points in time were opportunities to shape attitudes, values, convictions, and behaviors in

His followers by illuminating the ways in which those characteristics became obstacles to success. Jesus delighted in being
playful in some of His exhortation. He poked his disciples a
bit, saying, "Why do you look at the speck of sawdust in your
brother's eye and pay no attention to the plank in your own
eye? How can you say to your brother, 'Let me take the speck
out of your eye,' when all the time there is a plank in your own
eye? You hypocrite, first take the plank out of your own eye,
and then you will see clearly to remove the speck from your
brother's eye" (Matthew 7:3-5). Jesus knew human nature; he
recognized our tendency to look for flaws and faults in others
first—to consider the many ways in which others create barriers
before ever considering our own role in the system. Through
this playful hyperbole, Christ essentially cautions disciples to
examine their own inner convictions, attitudes, desires, and
actions to check for ways that these personal characteristics or
habits might in fact be holding self or others back.

On another occasion, Christ taught more explicitly,

> "And if anyone causes one of these little ones who believe in me
> to sin, it would be better for him to be thrown into the sea with a
> large millstone tied around his neck. If your hand causes you to
> sin, cut it off. It is better for you to enter life maimed than with
> two hands to go into hell, where the fire never goes out. And if
> your foot causes you to sin, cut it off. It is better for you to enter
> life crippled than to have two feet and be thrown into hell. And
> if your eye causes you to sin, pluck it out. It is better for you to
> enter the kingdom of God with one eye than to have two eyes
> and be thrown into hell, where 'their worm does not die, and

*the fire is not quenched.' Everyone will be salted with fire. Salt is
good, but if it loses its saltiness, how can you make it salty again?
Have salt in yourselves, and be at peace with each other"* (Mark
9:42-50).

I can't imagine a clearer teaching on removing obstacles! Our
tendency is to read this passage as if looking out a window,
evaluating and judging "those people" and their issues while
ignoring the planks in our own eyes. Christ calls us to hold
the Word up like a mirror and to evaluate ourselves in light
of his truth and conviction. Serving Leaders humbly accept
Christ's teaching and prayerfully examine themselves as David
did when he prayed, "Search me, O God, and know my heart;
test me and know my anxious thoughts. See if there is any of-
fensive way in me, and lead me in the way everlasting" (Psalm
139:23-24). Anything that gets in the way of the leader's personal growth and development, or impedes others in the organization becomes an obstacle to success. Such barriers include
but are not limited to sin, negative attitudes, self-serving behavior, power and control issues, stinginess, poor communication, unrealistic expectations, ineffective functional structures, and inadequate equipment and resources.

Spend some focused time in prayer asking God to illuminate
obstacles that you have inadvertently created which stand in
the way of other people's success. These obstacles might be attitudes; they might be specific behaviors; they might be ways in
which you withdraw or neglect to act. Ask select co-workers,
team members, ministry associates, key leaders, and volunteers to give you feedback regarding obstacles they perceive.

Pray that God grants you the humility to receive and process their feedback with integrity. Remember, it's not a sign of weakness to experience an obstacle or growing edge; it is a sign of strength to take action to overcome it.

Like a boulder on the highway, many obstacles are glaringly obvious—if not to the leader, then certainly to the followers. Some obstacles are more insidious and ingrained. These obstacles pertain to the limitations that hold followers or emerging leaders back; things like lack of confidence, low self-esteem, feelings of inadequacy. Encouragement, compassion, empathy, exhortation, and admonishment become hallmarks of a Serving Leader's relationships with others. Serving Leaders come alongside others in order to be channels of Christ's love and grace, offering the kind of agape love that invites others to grow beyond and overcome their own obstacles. In this way, such leaders function as obstacle-removers and Blaze the Trail for new pathways on the journey.

Other obstacles exist within the systems and structures of an organization. Things like communication breakdowns, multi-tiered decision-making channels, complicated reporting structures, processes that delay purchases, unclear policies and procedures all make the day-to-day life in the workplace tiring and frustrating. Relieving the tedium and streamlining systems and processes become relatively simple ways to remove obstacles and free the people up for greater efficiency and fruitfulness in their work and ministry.

✟ Theological Foundations

Look at any great organization and you'll find great leaders. Strong leadership forms the bedrock for a thriving community of people. Strong leaders are integral to the success and sustainability of any institution. As I study and become acquainted with organizations and their leaders across all sectors of society, **I'm distressed to discover how often the greatness of the leader is touted over against the collective greatness of the people**. Consider how often this priority reversal is true even in churches and non-profit organizations. The people in the organization, from "middle management" down to the grassroots are but the collective shadow of the great leaders. No one sets out to structure things that way, but somehow it happens. This inherent ethos suggests that people remain in the shadow of leaders; it conjures images of the great grassroots of an organization paling in comparison to its stellar leaders. It implies that the greatness of the organization (structures, systems, processes) and her leaders is paramount and her people are secondary.

I find the following to be a better philosophy: **Serving Leaders not only serve a "Great Purpose," they also serve the "Great People" who do the daily work of ministry**. A Serving Leader is nothing if s/he is not a people-developer and releaser. Serving Leaders activate the best in an organization by activating the best in its people and releasing tier after tier of leaders; removing obstacles to their success so that they can flourish, both individually and collectively.

When you pause to think about trail-blazing and the leader's role, what comes to your mind? Reflect on the mental images before you. For many of us, scenes come to mind that capture this action: epic war movies featuring generals leading troops into battle; eminent scientists paving the way toward a cure for diseases; creative engineers unleashing innovative computing technology; an athlete establishing a new world record. All of these images and more depict individuals who possess unique courage, charisma, skills, talents, training, and ingenuity out in front of "the pack." The leader assumes her position at the pinnacle, leading the masses through command and control who follow into a preferred future. The leader takes the helm, with the followers in tow. The same is true in most organizations. There are **leaders**, and there are **followers**; everyone knows who is who. We visualize that typical scenario in the following graphic:

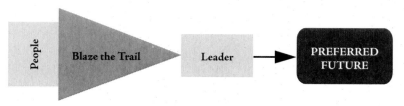

In this organizational make-up, the leader possesses sole responsibility for trail-blazing. All alone, out in front, the leader charts the course, establishes direction, steps out, and hopes the people follow. This leader carries a heavy burden that includes casting vision, engendering buy-in and support, facilitating culture shift, dealing with resistance, and championing change. This leader must constantly look over her shoulder to ascertain who is following, who is straggling, who is resisting, who has left the pack. Often progress becomes a "push and pull" struggle in which the group takes one step back for every two steps forward. That view is the admittedly cynical one, of course. But even the best case scenario finds the leader blazing the trail, calling over her shoulder to the willing followers, "Come on, Y'All! Who's with me?"

Consider an alternative scenario, as depicted below:

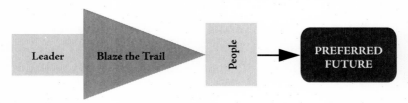

In this representation, the leader assumes the role of **facilitator/coach**, and ultimately the people Blaze the Trail, leading the way collectively for the organization. In this position, the leader functions as cheer-leader, exhorter, encourager, dream-releaser, vision-caster, team-builder, strengths-finder. Note that on an organizational chart, the leader might **positionally** occupy the place at the top of the pyramid on paper and still help to set the vision and strategy, but **functionally** s/he behaves and leads from the humble posture of supportive guidance. (We refer you back to the chapter on Upend the Pyramid.)

As you pause to think about organizational leadership and trail-blazing from this perspective, what visual images come to mind? Reflect for a moment. We picture runners at the start of a marathon race. When the starting gun sounds, the mass of competitors sets out as one body, sure of the direction and objective, clear on the course, properly trained and prepared. The metaphor quickly breaks down, obviously, because in a marathon, individual runners compete for the prize and strive to improve on personal best times. We love the image, however, of a group of people embarking on a significant, focused course together. Picture your organization blazing a trail with the grassroots leading the way as in a marathon. In this portrayal, the leader of the organization would be running also, but behind or alongside the pack—coaching, encouraging, exhorting, offering course corrections, guiding, and offering directives where appropriate. **This connotation of shared, collaborative leadership lies at the heart of Serving Leadership.**

This type of trail-blazing leadership requires significant strength in the top-level leader. These leaders are no less talented, gifted, charismatic, educated, trained, intelligent, wise, and shrewd than their counterparts who lead from positions of power and authority at the top of an organizational pyramid. **Serving Leaders are strong leaders.** A Serving Leader's strength is demonstrated with love and their actions are fueled by the strength Christ provides (see the chapter Build on Strength). These leaders are capable of making hard decisions, willing to exercise courage, earn the respect of the people in the organizations, and build successful ministries and initiatives. **Serving Leadership is not "soft" leadership.** Serving Leadership achieves greater results than would ever be possible through one individual or a small executive team by harnessing and releasing the energy and potential of all the people in the organization. In many respects this approach calls for greater strength and conviction than leading through conventional methods of command and control. Command and control seems easier because it focuses on tasks and strategic objectives rather than on people. People create messes and relationships are "messy." We believe it's simply easier to just "get stuff done." It's precisely the messiness of people and relationships that cries out for a different approach. Building authentic relationships, equipping, and releasing people to work from their strengths and potential actually streamlines organizational efficiency and productivity. **As leaders learn to become equippers rather than "doers of all significant things," the people of the organization collectively Blaze the Trail "full steam ahead."** Equipping is not easy, but it is that simple.

Daniel Goleman, Ph.D., has studied organizational behavior and leadership and published widely on the competency of emotional intelligence.[37] In his research on successful leaders of prominent organizations, Goleman discovered, "close to 90 percent of their success in leadership was attributable to emotional intelligence. To sum up: For star performance in all jobs, in every field, emotional competence is twice as important as purely cognitive abilities. For success at the highest lev-

---

37 Goleman defines emotional competence as "a learned capability based on emotional intelligence that results in outstanding performance at work... Our emotional intelligence determines our potential for learning the practical skills that are based on its five elements: self-awareness, motivation, self-regulation, empathy, and adeptness in relationships. Our emotional competence shows how much of that potential we have translated into on-the-job capabilities." [Daniel Goleman, Working with Emotional Intelligence, (Bantam Books, 1998), 24-25.]

els, in leadership positions, emotional competence accounts for virtually the entire advantage."[38] Goleman makes a "hard case for soft skills." The very attributes that many leaders dismiss as too "soft" or "touchy feely" are the ones that make or break a person's leadership and even make or break the organization. Serving Leaders who successfully Blaze the Trail exhibit high emotional intelligence. Placing a priority on teaching, training, and removing obstacle is part of the total package.

One of the many ways that leaders can adopt this mature trailblazing posture is by offering supportive guidance. **While offering supportive guidance, leaders both deflect credit to others and willingly receive the blame for failures while removing all the obstacles for a follower to succeed.**[39] In his book Good to Great, Jim Collins describes what he calls a "Level 5 Leader." Collins writes, "Level 5 leaders look out the window to apportion credit to factors outside themselves when things go well (and if they cannot find a specific person or event to give credit to, they credit good luck). At the same time, they look in the mirror to apportion responsibility, never blaming bad luck when things go poorly."[40] Collins' description of Level 5 leaders mirrors Jennings and Stahl-Wert's Serving Leader composite. When people in your organization know that you won't be looking out the window for someone else to blame for bumps in the road nor preening in front of the mirror when the road runs smoothly, then everyone main-

---

38 Ibid, 34.
39 Dr. Chris Hardy explored this understanding of supportive guidance during his doctoral project, and then he and I (Elizabeth) further developed the concept during our The Equipping Leader 3-part course.
40 Jim Collins, Good to Great, (New York: HarperCollins, 2001), 35.

tains a greater sense of "we're in this together." Collins wisely observes, "Strangely, the window and the mirror do not reflect objective reality. Everyone outside the window points inside, directly at the Level 5 leader, saying, 'He was the key; without his guidance and leadership, we would not have become a great company.' And the Level 5 leader points right back out the window and says, 'Look at all the great people and good fortune that made this possible; I'm a lucky guy.' They're both right, of course. But the Level 5s would never admit that fact."[41]

Remove Obstacles

Ponder for a moment the obstacles that currently exist in your life, ministry, relationships, work. What barriers stand in the way of greater fulfillment and/or accomplishment? Take a moment and list some of the obstacles you see.

_____

_____

_____

_____

_____

Consider your list. Did you name **personal** obstacles, **organizational** obstacles, or obstacles that you recognize as impediments for **other people** in your sphere of influence? Many leaders name personal obstacles. We're conditioned to think that way because often our inherited leadership models focus on the leader first. Success of the organization becomes

---

41 Ibid.

predicated on success of the leader. Leaders are groomed for personal advancement—they seek promotion and "better and brighter" opportunities; others esteem their drive and ambition. Often a position in a particular organization becomes the means of rising along a chosen career path. Top-level leaders carry the heavy burden of organizational success on their shoulders. If the organization succeeds, they succeed; if the organization fails, they are failures. Such leaders view anything or anyone that impedes personal or organizational progress as an obstacle. Even in the Church, competition among people and departments for position and resources, "turfism," and protective postures all serve to create personal, inter-personal, and organizational barriers to achieving the mission. Other people often become used by the leader as tools or resources to advance personal agenda or merely to grow the organization. People become cogs in the organizational machinery.

If you're like me, it's easy to define personal obstacles as anything or anyone that gets in **my** way. **Serving Leaders grow in their ability to view personal obstacles as anything that inhibits someone else in their progress.** Scripture makes plain, "Two are better than one, because they have a good return for their work; If one falls down, his friend can help him up. But pity the man who falls and has no one to help him up! Also, if two lie down together, they will keep warm. But how can one keep warm alone? Though one may be overpowered, two can defend themselves. A cord of three strands is not quickly broken" (Ecclesiastes 4:9-12). Two are better than one, and three are even better because they can equip each other and remove obstacles for each other. Such leaders recognize that they themselves may in fact be the obstacle that stands in someone else's way, and so they constantly seek feedback from others in order to assess the impact of their personal behaviors on others.

In your leadership role, think about ways in which you, personally, create obstacles for others without even knowing it. Obstacles to others' growth and development, obstacles to their promotion or advancement, obstacles to their fruitfulness in their work and mission. What attitudes, behaviors, or actions come to mind? What have you learned from others' feedback?

_____

_____

_____

_____

_____

As leaders, we unconsciously and inadvertently place barriers in the paths of our team members and others in the organization. The following table contrasts a few (not an exhaustive list) critical success factors with select barriers to success for team members and key leaders in any organization. Study each section of the table and place a check-mark beside the practices you consistently demonstrate. Then, in the large box to the left of the shaded list, create an action step to guide you in adding or further developing one of those Serving Leader practices. Next, in the large box to the left of the bottom section, create an action step to guide you in overcoming a behavior that creates obstacles for others as you serve alongside them in ministry.

ACTION STEP (You will further develop): _____ _____ _____ _____	You are readily available and "part of the team" You communicate clearly and regularly, using a variety of media You meet regularly 1:1 to provide mentoring/ coaching for team members You resist micro-management You share information freely and proactively You ensure needed resources are provided; such as print and web-based media, education, training, dollars, tools, etc. You live out a "Theology of Abundance"
ACTION STEP (You will overcome): _____ _____ _____ _____	You are largely inaccessible to team members You communicate infrequently and/or impersonally (e.g. memos, emails) You meet with team members primarily to provide directives or just to "check in" You have a hand in majority of initiatives You hold info close and shares with select others on a "need to know" basis You gauge resource availability based on budget or other constraints You live out a "Theology of Scarcity"

Assess where you stand. Show the clean list to your team members or key leaders in your organization and invite them to give you feedback. Compare your personal assessment with theirs. Most leaders are blind to the ways in which they impose obstacles to others' success, and most teammates and followers feel too inhibited to provide feedback that might help leaders to grow. You have likely checked more boxes in the top section of the table, but your people may see a different picture. Don't be afraid to receive this feedback—growing in self-awareness will allow you to Build on Strengths and overcome weaknesses that will lead to both personal and organizational transformation as you become a more effective leader.

 (Visit www.johnstahlwert.com/TSL **for podcast # 9 on "Build on Strength."**)

Often leaders hide behind protective mechanisms put in place to ensure personal survival. Leaders stand behind accomplishment and achievement—a kind of personal shield designed to communicate worth and value. Alternatively, **Serving Leaders live into the biblical paradox, secure in the knowledge that to protect your value, you must give it all away.** For many, this paradox proves hardest to live into. Leaders fear that if they teach, train, equip, and release people into the work of ministry that they will in the process work themselves out of a job. God gave leaders to the Body of Christ for the equipping of the saints (Ephesians 4:11, 12). The Word reveals that the natural result of equipped persons includes unity in the faith, knowledge of the Son of God, maturity, the fullness of Christ, and the Body built up in love as each part does its work (see Ephesians 4:13-16). Why would a church fire a leader who was a catalyst for that kind of amazing, transformative, life-giving growth? On the contrary, may their tribe increase!

 (Visit www.johnstahlwert.com/TSL **for podcast #10 on "Awakening the People of God."**)

✎₇ Key Behaviors and Practices

Following are some key behaviors and practices that you might consider adopting as you seek to more fully embody the Serving Leader Powerful Action, Blaze the Trail. After reading this chapter, you may be thinking, **HOW** do I become a leader who is a dynamic trail-blazer, an effective teacher and obstacle-remover? We hope you find some helpful suggestions here. You may also find it beneficial to discuss your key learnings and "ah-ha's" with a trusted mentor or coach. S/he can assist you in considering behavior modifications, encourage you to take risks, and challenge you to stretch outside your comfort zone.

With your team, staff, or key leaders:

* Schedule a session during which you brainstorm and list obstacles that currently exist personally, inter-personally, and organizationally.
* Narrow the list by consensus to one that seems relatively complete and comprehensive.
* Re-write the list into assessment form, such as a list of behaviors to check off or a list of behavioral statements that could be evaluated with a Lickert scale.
* Provide an assessment to each person to complete on themselves.
* Invite each person to ask 3 different people to evaluate them using the assessment as a means of providing feedback.
* Schedule coaching sessions with each person to talk about what they learned and discovered.

As a team:

* Determine means and methods for working to overcome the personal, inter-personal, and organizational obstacles that you identified.
* Establish accountability structures and benchmarks to help you monitor progress toward these goals.

Ask each person on your team or staff to make a list of resources that they need in order to grow personally and professionally, to better perform their work; and a "dream list" of resources they would need if they were to take their work to the next level or realize an unmet dream or vision. Sit down with each person and discuss their resource needs. Work together to develop a plan and process for obtaining these resources.

Evaluate your training programs and processes. Are you adequately training your team, staff, and volunteers? Develop a plan to hone strengths and to fill in gaps. Establish a timeline for providing regular training for each of these groups.

A Real-Life Story
By Rachel Sosebee, director of ministry initiatives at St. Paul Lutheran Church in Columbus, Ohio

I didn't know what I was getting myself into. I was 23 and just hired as the Director of Ministry Initiatives for a traditional congregation. Most of them didn't know what to think of me. Some thought I might be another pastor, some thought I was

their new youth director, others thought I was another sec-
retary. Some just thought I was a waste of money. What was I
supposed to do? I was charged with transforming this mostly
traditional Lutheran congregation into a culture that trained,
discipled, and equipped people to do ministry inside and outside the church. What did that mean?

There I was finishing my Masters of Lay Ministry called to "assist
in broadening our base of ministry by leading all who are committed to creating and sustaining efforts that serve, support,
and engage people in spiritual growth." I had no idea where to
start. I can only imagine what the church thought.

Thank God for Pastor Matt! He equipped me to be the best
Director of Ministries I could be by casting the vision of
equipping ministries, going with me to numerous workshops
and debriefing with me, and coaching me into discovering my
leadership capabilities. He fought battles with the skeptics,
helped me find opportunities to grow, let me test things out,
and was simply there for whatever I needed as I felt my way
blindly through the first couple years of discovering my passion for equipping and growing disciples!

In the beginning I made official appointments to talk with Pastor Matt because my job description said that I was to meet
with the pastor. At the first meeting, Matt put on his coaching
hat and told me he had an open door policy and whenever I
needed to, we could talk. He saw part of his job as a leader to
be a sounding board, asking good questions, and just getting
out of the way so people could do what they loved to do. Hav-

ing an open door for people to pop in and discuss their problems, ideas, passions, or whatever happened to be on their mind was just part of the job.

My first year, I didn't waste any time getting into the mix of things happening at church. I invited myself to every official meeting I could and tried to get to know the movers and the shakers and anyone that I could. One morning, I was in a women's Bible study meeting. This was not my first meeting with them, but I was still new to them. I didn't know it, but I was about to step on a hornet's nest.

I had just announced to the congregation that we were implementing a ministry year. This would be an official start and stop for ministry teams and would include an invitation for leaders to stay in their current ministry or to pass their position on. The woman leading the funeral dinners told me she did not want to do the dinners anymore, so I went to the women's meeting to see if any of them wanted to take over the ministry. They hemmed, hawed, and made excuses. I finally said, "Seeing no one, I'll seek someone else" and asked for suggestions. I did not realize that even if no one stepped up officially to serve as leader for the funeral ministry, they saw it as *their* ministry and someone would do it. The converstaion quickly got out of control. I was sucked into explaining (well, more like defending) this new ministry direction and my position at church, and finally finished the meeting with the women criticizing people of my generation not having time for church. I tried to find a graceful way out of the conversation. Finding none, I just thanked them for their comments and got out of the room as fast as I could.

After a few moments to compose myself in the restroom, I went into my office and tried to work. Not being able to mentally leave that room, I walked down the hall to Matt's office and asked if he had a few minutes.

Well, the few minutes turned into an hour or so because I got my first situational, real life Family Systems Theory lesson. Through stories, personal experiences, debriefing, and asking questions, Matt explained systems theory to me and helped me see how these women were not necessarily complaining about me or what I was doing, but mourning for how the world had changed. He explained how it was an opportunity to walk with them, empathize, minister and care for them, share the vision of what we were trying to accomplish, and bless them. All that from a, "What in the world happened?" debriefing.

That conversation has happened a million times over. Just pick the topic and Pastor Matt has played the perfect gym wall off which to bounce ideas, experiences, bewilderments, and joys. He asks great questions and shares experiences that make me think.

Over the almost seven years we have worked together, our conversations haven't changed. Except, that now they bounce much more naturally between what is happening at St. Paul, cooking (a mutual hobby), the nature of the Holy Spirit, and learning from each other's strengths. Pastor Matt still has an open door policy and he shares his insights gained through experiences, study of the Scripture, and favorite books and speakers. And I'm still soaking it up like a thick piece of bread in a really good bowl of soup.

Closing Thought and Questions for Reflection

The danger of Blazing the Trail is getting out ahead of Jesus. The temptation to "make things happen" without waiting for God's clear direction will always be there, particularly when ministry is evaluated on production (attendance, number of programs, financial giving, etc.) rather than transformed lives (people becoming more and more like Jesus). Prayer should permeate the life of the church, particularly when needing God's wisdom (James 3:17) for future direction, teaching, and removing obstacles. What good is it to blaze a trail that Jesus has not gone down before you?

* What makes your church, Christian organization, or school distinctive?
* In light of this, what is your organization's distinctive mission?
* How can you better teach and remove obstacles for others on your team so that this distinctive mission is better advanced through them?

Build on Strength

Now to each one the manifestation of the Spirit is given for the common good... All these are the work of one and the same Spirit, and he gives them to each one, just as he deter-mines... But in fact God has arranged the parts of the body, every one of them, just as he wanted them to be.
(1 Corinthians 12:7,11,18)

Definition: Serving leaders Build on Strength by arranging each person in the team, the business, and the community to contribute according to what s/he does best. This focus improves everyone's performance and solidifies teams by aligning the strengths of many people.

Paradoxes: To address your weaknesses, focus on your strengths. You can't become the best unless others do, too.

"Success is achieved by developing our strengths, not by eliminating our weaknesses."
Marilyn vos Savant

"Most leaders spend time trying to get others to think highly of them, when instead they should try to get their people to think more highly of themselves. It's wonderful when the people believe in their leader. It's more wonderful when the leader believes in their people! You can't hold a man down without staying down with him... There are two ways of exerting one's strength: one is pushing down, the other is pulling up."

Booker T. Washington

 Narrative

"The problem as I see it, is that we have a lot of Chiefs and not enough regular Indians."

Pastor Greg stopped talking, teed up his golf ball, and then hit it as hard as he could. He knew instantly that he was in for trouble. The ball started out straight but then hooked left into the woods that lined that side of the fairway. "Ugh! Not again... That's exactly what I didn't want to do," he bemoaned.

Bill Anderson, the clerk of the church board, stepped up to the tee and said, "You know, if you slowed down your swing and didn't try to kill it every time you might have more success." Bill modeled what he was talking about by swinging smoothly and following through the shot. The ball launched out like a rocket and landed far down the middle of the fairway.

"You have been doing that all day," quipped Greg. Bill simply smiled. It wasn't often that he got to "preach" to his young pastor.

The two started walking down the fairway. Bill continued, "Greg you're right about the board members all having strong opinions and personalities, but if you can get their strengths working together, I think we could do something wonderful for the Lord. Let's find your ball."

After a brief search, Bill discovered the ball under a pine tree. Greg decided to play it, and after taking an awkward stance, chipped the ball back onto the fairway. "That's easy to say, and another thing to do…" he said. "A lot of these board members run their own businesses and aren't used to doing things together."

Bill replied, "Yes, it's hard to lead a bunch of leaders. But you can do it." They reached Greg's ball. "Now—this time swing with a nice even tempo, keep your eye on the ball, and remember to follow through."

Greg did as instructed. He felt something he hadn't felt in a long time. He had hit "the sweet spot." Without swinging hard at all, the ball took off as if shot from a cannon. He caught Bill's smiling approval. "Thanks… How much do I owe you?" he said jokingly.

"Nothin'," laughed Bill. "But there is something you can do for me."

"What's that?"

"Help this church board slow down its swing and find its sweet spot. OK?"

Greg looked at Bill. With fresh understanding, he said, "OK. Thanks for the lesson."

 **Chapter Overview**

Are you a "glass half empty" person or a "glass half full" person? When you look at your life, when you consider your ministry and your work, do you first see the gaps between where you are and where you want to be; or do you focus on your strengths, recognizing and affirming the gifts and abilities God has given you? Our God is a creative Gift-giver—the Author of infinite possibilities! Regardless of how you tend to view your "glass," God invites you to focus on His best for you and to cultivate that "best" in yourself in order that you might be a catalyst for others to develop their best.

Ultimately, Christian leadership is people-development. It's all about other people. Any other pursuit mocks the Gospel and God's call. Christian leadership is not about self-aggrandizement and making a name for oneself; it's not about growing the church or organization; it's not a career in which one climbs a "corporate ladder." Christian leaders—Serving Leaders—love, equip, and release God's people; and invite others into the journey in Christ. Christian leadership, pure and simple, is a more highly visible expression of discipleship and disciple-making. Strong leadership is predicated on love. We hope this chapter inspires you to lean into the strength God provides and to more fully become a people-releaser for the sake of Christ's mission in the world.

📖 Biblical Foundations

God's Word vividly illustrates our Heavenly Father as Giver of good gifts. James writes, "Every good and perfect gift is from above, coming down from the Father of the heavenly lights, who does not change like shifting shadows" (James 1:17). Strength is one of God's many good gifts to God's people. The Triune God exists in strength and imparts strength to those who are called according to God's purposes. Not only does God impart strength as a gift, but God strengthens us through the indwelling Holy Spirit so that we might be empowered to live and serve faithfully. Scripture paints a picture of strength flowing from God the Source to and through individual persons and faith communities. God is Strength; God imparts strength as gracious gift; God strengthens the Priesthood of Believers.

In the face of human limitations and weaknesses, isn't it a comfort to realize that the God we know and serve is Strength? Depending on the translation you read, you will find over 40 references throughout the Old Testament to God as stronghold or refuge. "The LORD is good, a stronghold in the day of trouble, and He knows those who take refuge in Him" (Nahum 1:7) [NASV] (cf. Joel 4:16; Psalm 9:9, 27:1, 37:39-40). A stronghold cannot be breached, moved, or destroyed. God, in essence, is Strength and Fortitude. Many scriptural names for God speak to the attribute of strength; following are a few representatives in the Hebrew: As Strength, God is known as Ma'oz; as Mighty Creator, God is Elohim; El Shadday is God Almighty; The Lord My Rock is Yahweh Tsuri.

Strength is one aspect of God's being; Scripture also depicts God's action in strong metaphors. David wrote, "For you [God] have been my refuge, a strong tower against the foe" (Psalm 61:3). Solomon picked up the refrain, "The name of the LORD is a strong tower; the righteous run to it and are safe" (Proverbs 18:10). Scripture is rife with references to God's strong Name, strong arm, great strength, and unsurpassing greatness. God does not exist remotely and isolated in God's strength, but rather invites believers into His strong presence and imparts strength to those who trust Him.

In the chapters Run to Great Purpose and Raise the Bar, we considered the glorious reality of our identity in Christ. Hopefully you drew encouragement and invigoration from meditating on the Scriptures related to your life in Christ. In his letter to the Ephesians, Paul calls out to God, "I pray that out of his [God the Father's] glorious riches he may strengthen you with power through his Spirit in your inner being" (Eph. 3:16). The Heavenly Father, who is Strength, imparts the same to you and to me. Sometimes when we think of "strength," we're guilty of focusing too narrowly on the concept. In our mind, we picture harsh images of steel cables, sterile structures, power and control, rigid boundaries. We are delighted to discover that the specific phrase "the LORD is my strength and song" occurs in three distinct places in Scripture with three separate individuals taking up the refrain. We're captivated by this uplifting linkage between **strength** and **song**. Moses and the Israelites sang, "The LORD is my strength and my song; he has become my salvation" (Exodus 15:2). The psalmist echoes, "The LORD is my strength and my song; he has become my salvation" (Psalm 118:14). Isaiah joins in the chorus, "Surely God is my salvation; I will trust and not be afraid. The LORD, the LORD, is my strength and my song; he has become my salvation" (Isiah 12:2). God's gracious and life-giving strength pours into us by the Holy Spirit and then overflows out of us through joyous expressions of praise and service to others. Strength resides within us as a wellspring of life, a fountain of joy and delight. Strength actually becomes a playful aspect of our being as we draw upon it with gladness and allow it to fuel our God-given gifts as if by song.

God uniquely gifts individual believers to fulfill their various roles and functions in the Body of Christ. Thank God we aren't left to try to use those gifts in our own strength! **Spiritual gifts and God's strength come to us** wrapped in the same package. Peter admonished, "Each one should use whatever gift he has received to serve others, faithfully administering God's grace in its various forms. If anyone speaks, he should do it as one speaking the very words of God. If anyone serves, he should do it with the strength God provides, so that in all things God may be praised through Jesus Christ. To him be the glory and the power for ever and ever. Amen" (1 Peter 4:10, 11, emphasis added). Peter doesn't directly reference God as "strength and song" and yet I hear that harmony providing beautiful background music for his exhortation.

Our Strength: God's Gift and Call
Your strength, my strength, is God's gift. As Serving Leaders, we must cling to this truth. As the days, months, years go by we often default to a reliance on self, skills, and savvy rather than

on the indwelling Spirit of God who sustains and strengthens. Why is it that for so many of us in ministry we reach a "critical mass" of knowledge and experience and then become deceived into believing it's sufficient? Why is it that early in our walk with Christ we experience a robust personal worship life and then somehow one day we start neglecting spiritual disciplines as if our "tank" is perpetually full? This trap is especially easy for ministry professionals to fall into. After all, we've been to seminary or Bible college, we've attended conference after conference, we feel a certain confidence in our spiritual maturity, others look up to us as wise "experts."

The Apostle Paul's confidence was rooted in Christ, "I can do everything through him [Christ] who gives me strength" (Philippians 4:13). Christ Jesus himself affirmed the inverse, "I am the vine; you are the branches. If a man remains in me and I in him, he will bear much fruit; apart from me you can do nothing" (John 15:5, emphasis added). Isaiah the Prophet paints a startling image of the futility of self-reliance, "All of us have become like one who is unclean, and all our righteous acts are like filthy rags; we all shrivel up like a leaf, and like the wind our sins sweep us away" (Isaiah 64:6). We are incapable of righteous acts, sufficient service, apart from God. Those efforts are anemic at best and "filthy rags" at worst.

God presents strength as one of many biblical paradoxes. Paul knew that he preached the Gospel, "not with words of human wisdom, lest the cross of Christ be emptied of its power... Has not God made foolish the wisdom of the world?... For the foolishness of God is wiser than man's wisdom, and the weakness of God is stronger than man's strength" (I Corinthians 1:17, 20c, 25). Clearly, God calls believers to rely on God's strength; not our own, God-given strength appears weak or foolish by human standards and yet it reflects the creative power that birthed our universe and the resurrection power that shook the earth and rolled back the grave stone.

At this point, you may rightly argue, "but God created humans in God's image and endowed them with a certain amount of innate human strength. Doesn't God require us to invest it? What are we to do with it?" God provides the answer: "Hear, O Israel: 'The LORD our God, the LORD is one. **Love** the LORD your God with all your heart and with all your soul and with all your **strength**" (Deuteronomy 6:4-5, emphasis added). When an expert in the law (strong in his own strength?) tested Jesus with a question about the greatest commandment, Jesus replied, "'Love the LORD your God with all your heart and with all your soul and with all your mind.' This is the first and greatest commandment. And the second is like it: 'Love your neighbor as yourself.' All the Law and the Prophets hang on these two commandments" (Matthew 22:37-40). **So what are we to do with our human strength? Love**. Pure and simple. **Love God and others** out of the wellspring of your human strength; **serve** out of the wellspring of Christ's strength—a gift of God, empowered through the Holy Spirit.

Stop and think about that statement for a moment. Love with your strength! As we pray for Christ's Kingdom to come and his will to be done, **let us pray that people would learn to love with their strength**. Oh how Christ must weep as we daily misuse our strength. We employ our strength for personal gain, to trample on others, to wage war, to press personal agendas, to manipulate, to dominate, to intimidate... the list goes on. We misuse our strength when we think of ourselves more highly than we ought (Romans 12:3), serving from our own limited resources. Leaders miss the mark when they labor out of their strength, rather than love. The call of Christ is to love—love God and love others. God endows us with strength—God's own strength—in order that we might love fiercely, love fervently, love ferociously—love strongly. One might argue that labor is a loving act. Indeed it can be. Labor becomes abundantly loving when it is fueled by God, the source of love, for the purpose of equipping and releasing others to become loving servants themselves.

God weaves together love and strength and presents it graciously to believers in the form of call. **A call** is a summons to heed God's voice and to participate in Christ's Kingdom; the call comes gift-wrapped in love and strength. Tragically, many individuals fail to hear God's voice; fail to recognize the call. One of my favorite biblical stories is found in Judges 6— Gideon's call. Gideon is an "every man" kind of guy—one with whom we can all relate.

Israel's suffering and oppression at the hands of Midian forms the context for Gideon's story. Basically, Midian ravaged and devastated Israel in every way imaginable. Forgetting God's deliverance and promises and forsaking authentic worship, Israel cowered and retreated in fear. We find Gideon threshing grain in a winepress in order to elude the Midian oppressors.

An angel of the Lord appears to Gideon in his hiding place. The angel greets him, "The LORD is with you, mighty warrior" (Judges 6:12b). The image conjured by that extraordinary salutation—picture Gideon startled (an understatement) and looking around to see whom this strange visitor might be addressing, is powerful. Gideon, apparently flustered and confused, can only muster a weak protest, "if the LORD is with us, why has all this happened to us?" (vs. 13a). God's response cuts to the heart of God's best for Gideon and speaks directly to the core of any believer who has ears to hear. "The LORD turned to him and said, 'Go in the strength you have and save Israel out of Midian's hand. Am I not sending you?' 'But Lord,' Gideon asked, 'how can I save Israel? My clan is the weakest in Manasseh, and I am the least in my family.' The LORD answered, 'I will be with you, and you will strike down all the Midianites together'" (vs. 14-16).

We know many people in the Body of Christ who have no idea who they are in God's eyes. That lack of awareness is a travesty! Serving Leaders are privileged to walk alongside people and help them learn to listen for God's voice. How many "mighty warriors" are out there who simply need to awaken to God's call on their lives? How many teachers, mentors of children and youth, community organizers, advocates, foster parents, small group leaders, providers of hospitality, visioncasters—the list is endless. Does it excite you to see yourself entering into prayer and discernment with another person in your sphere of influence and hearing God's voice declare to that person, "The LORD is with you, mentor of inner city children!" God's formula for success is simple; we see it in

Gideon's call narrative: God is present, God gives strength, God sends, God provides.[42] In the process of discerning a call, people often awaken to strengths and gifts not previously known. Serving Leaders Build on Strength as they journey with others toward hearing and answering a call.

God invites Serving Leaders to be "Barnabas" for the people in their community. The New Testament Barnabas' name literally means "Son of Encouragement." People can take spiritual gifts inventories and other assessments, and those tools are of great value. Of inestimable worth are the voices in the community calling forth the gifts and strengths of the people. As people live in and experience community together, they naturally observe and witness the various gifts at work in the Body. Serving Leaders function as "midwives," helping to bring forth the gifts of the Body, born in love. God provided the metaphor of Body in order to help us recognize the amazing ways God has gifted and strengthened the various parts in order to create a mature and unified whole. Paul writes,

---

42 The call narratives in Scripture tend to follow a common pattern. Typically, these accounts contain five key ingredients: 1) some sort of crisis during which God confronts the person; 2) God summons the person for some specific action or to deliver a pertinent message; 3) the person raises objections related to their perceived inadequacy for the task; 4) God promises help, often in the formula "I will be with you;" 5) the person asks for a sign to confirm God's call and commission. For example, see the calls of Gideon (Judges 6), the call of Moses (Exodus 3-4), Jeremiah (Jeremiah 1), Isaiah (Isaiah 6), and Ezekiel (Ezekiel 2-3). People today often experience the same sequence of events as they hear God's voice and wrestle with a sense of call. Serving Leaders play a significant role in shepherding these people as they discern God's call. Serving Leaders adopt the role of coach as they prayerfully and actively listen and ask probing questions in order to facilitate another person's discovery.

There are different kinds of gifts, but the same Spirit. There are different kinds of service, but the same Lord. There are different kinds of working, but the same God works all of them in all men.

Now to each one the manifestation of the Spirit is given for the common good. To one there is given through the Spirit the message of wisdom, to another the message of knowledge by means of the same Spirit, to another faith by the same Spirit, to another gifts of healing by that one Spirit, to another miraculous powers, to another prophecy, to another distinguishing between spirits, to another speaking in different kinds of tongues, and to still another the interpretation of tongues. All these are the work of one and the same Spirit, and he gives them to each one, just as he determines.

The body is a unit, though it is made up of many parts; and though all its parts are many, they form one body. So it is with Christ. For we were all baptized by one Spirit into one body— whether Jews or Greeks, slave or free—and we were all given the one Spirit to drink.

Now the body is not made up of one part but of many. If the foot should say, 'Because I am not a hand, I do not belong to the body,' it would not for that reason cease to be part of the body. And if the ear should say, 'Because I am not an eye, I do not belong to the body,' it would not for that reason cease to be part of the body. If the whole body were an eye, where would the sense of hearing be? If the whole body were an ear, where would the sense of smell be? But in fact God has arranged the parts in the body, every one of them, just as he wanted them to be. If they were all one part, where would the body be? As it is, there are many parts, but one body.

The eye cannot say to the hand, 'I don't need you!' And the head cannot say to the feet, 'I don't need you!' On the contrary, those parts of the body that seem to be weaker are indispensable, and the parts that we think are less honorable we treat with special honor. And the parts that are un-presentable are treated with special modesty, while our presentable parts need no special treatment. But God has combined the members of the body and has given greater honor to the parts that lacked it, so that there should be no division in the body, but that its parts should have equal concern for each other. If one part suffers, every part suffers with it; if one part is honored, every part rejoices with it (1 Corinthians 12:4-26).

Many strong parts comprise a healthy physical body. The same is true for the church or any other organization. Serving Leaders Build on Strength by helping the "ears" to hear and live into their roles; by assisting the "eyes" to become enlightened to their unique function; by exhorting the "heads" to adopt a humble posture and to equip the "feet." As the Body of Christ becomes strengthened and equipped, it matures. Paul affirms, "we will in all things grow up into him who is the Head, that is Christ. From him the whole body, joined and held together by every supporting ligament, grows and builds itself up in love, as each part does its work" (Ephesians 4:15,16).

Serving Leaders do well to recognize and cultivate their own strengths, but never toward a self-serving end. You can't become the best unless others do, too.

For the Sake of Others

Christian leaders—Serving Leaders—love, equip, and release God's people; and invite others into the journey in Christ. Robert Mulholland defines discipleship in his incredible book, Invitation to a Journey. He describes spiritual formation (discipleship) as a process of being conformed to the image of Christ for the sake of others.[43] **I can think of no better definition for Serving Leadership. Ultimately, a Serving Leader cultivates and hones personal strengths in order to catalyze that process in others. A Serving Leader embraces God's invitation to invest in other people in order to help them realize their full potential in Christ.** The reward for such selfless service is to someday hear God whisper well done, good and faithful servant. Serving Leaders don't seek the accolades of others, the denominational or organizational awards, their name on a plaque. A Serving Leader's legacy is never comprised of buildings, programs, ministries, or accomplishments. **A Serving Leader's legacy is people.** People, spiritually mature and engaged in building Christ's Kingdom, are the reward for a life of Serving Leadership. Paul knew and embraced this godly vision. "For what is our hope, our joy, or the crown in which we will glory in the presence of our Lord Jesus when he comes. Is it not you? Indeed, you are our glory and joy" (1 Thessalonians 2:19, 20). "Therefore, my broth-

---

43 M. Robert Mulholland, Jr, Invitation to a Journey: A Road Map for Spiritual Formation, (Downers Grove, IL: InterVarsity Press, 1993), 12.

ers, you whom I love and long for, my joy and crown, that is how you should stand firm in the Lord, dear friends!" (Philippians 4:1). The crown is not a trophy representative of accomplishing tasks and building empires; the crown is mature disciples of our Lord Jesus Christ who become loving, Serving Leaders themselves.

The temptation to Build on Strength by trying harder lures many leaders with its siren call. Serving Leaders Build on Strength through surrender—taking the and through falling into the strong arms of the One who provides life, love, and strength. Through Isaiah, God promises, "The LORD... gives strength to the weary and increases the power of the weak... those who hope in the LORD will renew their strength. They will soar on wings like eagles; they will run and not grow weary, they will walk and not be faint" (Isaiah 40:28-31). "So do not fear; for I am with you; do not be dismayed, for I am your God. I will strengthen you and help you; I will uphold you with my righteous right hand" (Isaiah 41:10). The phrase be strong and courageous occurs ten times in Scripture (Deuteronomy 31:6, 7, 23; Joshua 1:6,9, 18, 10:25; 1 Chronicles 22:13, 28:20; 2 Chronicles 32:7). God himself fuels you for this capacity. Build on the strength God gives and trust in the One who is Strength.

May our Lord Jesus Christ himself and God our Father, who loved us and by his grace gave us eternal encouragement and good hope, encourage your hearts and strengthen you in every good deed and word, (2 Thessalonians 2:16,17).

✝ Theological Foundations

To be clear, Serving Leaders do not Build on Strength to the exclusion of shoring up and overcoming weaknesses. Indeed, every human possesses limitations, faults, failings, shortcomings. Pursuing excellence requires paying attention to gaps as well as strengths; a process of maturation includes overcoming obstacles and transforming flaws. And so it is necessary to also look at one's weaknesses, at the weaknesses in one's organization—take a "serious moral inventory," as people in the Recovery Movement call it—and then take action to address those shortcomings.

But a focus on weaknesses to the exclusion of strengths quickly becomes demoralizing, discouraging, and self-defeating. We all have shortcomings, which must be admitted, addressed, and compensated for. Being part of a leadership community is the first and best way to address one's weaknesses; someone else is strong in precisely the way you are weak. We partner with others to forge whole and competent teams.

The reason we Build on Strengths is precisely because God designed us with certain capacities and passions that He wants to use to advance His kingdom. There is "better" work for us to do, as Mary and Martha learned in their journey as Jesus' followers, and we have a stewardship responsibility to discover what our "better" work is.

What God is Doing

In 1955, The Rev. Samuel Shoemaker moved to Pittsburgh, Pennsylvania to serve a final parish in his long life of ministry in the Episcopal Church. Sam had been Rector of the famous Calvary Episcopal Church in New York City for many years, had founded a magazine in 1927 called "God At Work," and had led Bill W. and Dr. Bob (the founders of Alcoholics Anonymous) to sobriety and to Christ. By Bill W. and Dr. Bob's own admission, Sam had given them the 12 Steps of Alcoholics Anonymous.

What Sam knew, and what he brought with him to Pittsburgh at the end of his years of ministry, was that most men and women felt cut off from their passion and gifting, and isolated from their true community. What is true, as a matter of fact, is that we cannot live in our calling if we don't live in the body—in true community.

Why is that true? It is true, because no one is well-rounded. And yet any meaningful task requires many skills to accomplish. If we are alone, we cannot focus on our strengths, because we must be "chief cook and bottle washer." **At the heart of "Build on Strength" is the theological understanding that God made us in such a way that we are essential to one another. We cannot be who we are to be if we are not connected to one another.** There are well-rounded teams of colleagues—each one playing to their strengths—but we cannot "Build on Strengths" alone.

In 1955, in a Time Magazine article written about Sam Shoemaker titled "God and Steel in Pittsburgh" Sam was quoted saying this:

> *The untapped conviction and belief in this city means more to it than all the coal in the hills and all the steel in the mills. If we can train and mobilize that force, Pittsburgh will become a spiritual pilot plant for America.*

Indeed. And this is true of all Christian communities, all gatherings of believers in all neighborhoods, cities, and nations. At the heart of "Build on Strength" is a call to true Christian community. With one another, we are able to discern what our true motivations and abilities are, what we're on earth to do, who we are called to co-labor with, and how—together—we can manifest the "spiritual pilot plant" Shoemaker spoke of. We don't "Build on Strengths" out of selfish motivation.

It isn't self-centered to seek to bring our best to the Body and there to link with the best of others. It is for the glory of God that we do this. It is for the advancement of His kingdom that we seek to discover what is our best, so we can lay our lives down meaningfully, impactfully, and in true serving leadership to one another - for the glory of God.

⌨ Key Behaviors and Practices

. . . .

Following are some key behaviors and practices that you might consider adopting as you seek to more fully embody the Serving Leader Powerful Action, Build on Strength. After reading this chapter, you may be thinking, **HOW** do I become a leader who is able to facilitate growth through honing strengths? We hope you find some helpful suggestions here. You may also find it beneficial to discuss your key learnings and "ah-ha's" with a trusted mentor or coach. S/he can assist you in considering behavior modifications, encourage you to take risks, and challenge you to stretch outside your comfort zone.

Assess your personal strengths using a tool such as Strengths-Finder 2.0.[44]

Provide copies of the StrengthsFinder book (or similar resource) to your team members or other leaders in your organization.

* Ask everyone to read the book and take the assessment. Set a due date.
* Schedule a meeting during which everyone shares the results of their assessment. Create a chart or other visual representation of the strengths of the entire team.

---

44 Tom Rath, StrengthsFinder 2.0: A New and Upgraded Edition of the On-line Test from Gallup's Now, Discover Your Strengths, (New York: Gallup Press, 2007). In addition to its helpful content, this book provides an access code and directs you to a website where you can take an online assessment of your strengths and receive a composite snapshot of your strengths make-up.

* As a team, discuss what you see in the composite representation related to the strengths balance on your team and
the implications for your organization's great purpose.
* Create a plan to better utilize the strengths of individual
members in order to strengthen the team and enhance
your mission.

Build time into your calendar and to-do list to affirm and celebrate the strengths you see in other people in the organization. Verbally call out these strengths, both 1:1 with individuals
and publicly during team meetings.

Identify three people on your team or in your organization
in whom you can intentionally invest, in order to help them
identify and build on their strengths. Schedule time this
month to meet with these people for the expressed purpose of
building on strength.

Schedule opportunities to teach (and preach if that is your
role) on gifts and strengths within the Body of Christ.

A Real-Life Story

by Pastor Dale W. Patterson, senior pastor at Hackberry Creek Church in Irving, Texas

....

Fire ants taught me a lesson on church leadership. Prior to my move from the upper Midwest to Texas more than twenty years ago, I had never seen a fire ant or a fire ant hill. That changed literally overnight. Fire ants are subterranean beasts that thrive in the challenging environs of Texas mesquite country. They are mean boogers—sorry, bugs—that take over your yard unless you wage a war of vigilance against them.

If by misfortune you should step on a nest or blockade a fire ant freeway, you will know why they are called "fire ants." If they carried flamethrowers and torched you, it could not burn any more than the wicked hell of one of their bites, let alone dozens of bites on an ankle.

We had a little thundershower one evening and I thought nothing of it other than that my yard would not need to be watered. But next morning as I walked out in the yard to retrieve my morning paper, several blackish volcano-like mounds had erupted in my yard. The little mountains were eight or ten inches tall each. Maliciously, I stomped on one of the volcanoes. My lesson in fire ants commenced immediately.

What seemed like ten thousand fire ants exploded into frenzied defensive action. Fortunately, I knew to get my foot and leg out of there and was spared the trauma of more fire ant bites.

Also I had a lesson in leadership and church growth. A fire ant hill has no structure, no support. They grow impressively overnight, but in truth there's not really much there but a few thousand angry fire ants. A few years later as a church planter I realized my church had become a fire ant hill.

How does one start a new church? Take a workshop, learn from others, then do what the experienced and the experts tell the church plant team to do. As a young pastor, I went to the hot workshop of the day, the Robert Schuller Institute for Successful Leadership. He was the church planting and leadership guru of that day. Something he told the conferees I have not forgotten: "Never put a banker or lawyer on your church decision-making board. They'll always find good reasons to say 'No' to any innovation."

I remembered that proverb when I put together the leadership team of the church I was in the process of planting. Church plants naturally attract risk-takers and entrepreneurs, and no surprise that's who I am as well. Therefore, when it came time to call forth leadership for our fledgling church start, we had a double-edged sword of sorts. First, we attracted entrepreneurs; that's who shows up as a pioneer in a non-established church. Second, when I looked for leaders, I looked most naturally for what I thought was a good leader—a decision-maker and make-things-happen person—and that means I looked for entrepreneurs like me. Our first leadership board was, therefore, all entrepreneurs. This was not in itself a crisis, but little did I know it was a formula for a fire ant hill congregation.

A leadership team of entrepreneurs is quick to roll the dice, make a decision, and get on with it. I remember fondly one of our decision-making principles: "You have to break a few eggs to make an omelet." We were going through eggs left and right, and much was starting - a fire ant hill in truth. The church took off, and we were quick to start one initiative after another. It was an energized, action-packed whirlwind of one idea after another. We were entrepreneurs in the best sense and worst sense of the word. But we were unaware of the fire ant hill rising up around us. We were also a bit blind to a possibility: Entrepreneurs like to start things, but they can struggle to finish things.

It began to dawn upon even the most dull of our entrepreneur-leadership team people when the conversation went like this:

> Leader A: Hey, at our last leader team meeting we decided to start such 'n' such. I don't think anybody's done anything about such 'n' such.
> Leader B: Yeah, why didn't that get done?
> Leader C: Because someone dropped the ball.
> Leader A: Who dropped the ball?
> Leader B: I can't remember who we said would do what!

We had built an impressive fire ant hill, but that's really all we had. We had a hive of activity, but nothing to give it structure. Our fire ant hill sprung up overnight, but it could just as easily have been crushed with a quick stomp. Then Providence intervened.

At the time, our fire ant hill church was in a hotbed of demographic expansion and corporate relocation in the metro

Dallas-Fort Worth area. Many major corporate headquarters relocating to the Dallas Fort Worth area came right to our immediate neighborhood. Inside those corporate headquarters were organization people, detail people, people who know about building structure. And those organizational people began to show up at our fire ant hill. With them came a foundation of expertise; no detail and corporate structure was too mundane for them.

But we still had a problem. Fire Ant Church was still run by the entrepreneurs. The strengths of our entrepreneurs had established a thriving new congregation, albeit with a lack of structure. It was time to add our strengths to the strengths of our organizational people who wandered into our fire ant hill. It was time to build upon our strengths.

Increasingly, when we summoned people to particular responsibilities, or created a leadership team, we looked for a healthy balance of appropriate gifts. Among the two most important polarities were entrepreneurial audacity on the one hand, and attention to system, structure, and accountability on the other. People's particular gifts and skill sets became more and more the focus.

Fire ant hills never build an infrastructure to support them. But we learned that while we liked the energy of the fire ant hill, we needed to build structure into our systems, not to stifle, but to accomplish a solid ministry presence. Yet even as we folded organization-people into our leadership team, we remained committed to stay strongly entrepreneurial.

Schuller's caution about empowering naysayers has never left our congregational DNA. So when church policies and procedures were implemented, they never were an end in themselves, but a means to help us accomplish our ministry. That commitment has helped transform a fire ant hill to a fire ant hill with a superstructure. That makes all the difference amidst the challenges and crushing forces of change and ministry in our world today.

Closing Thought and Questions for Reflection

Just as every person who has ever lived has a unique fingerprint, so each church, Christian organization, school, etc. has its own unique fingerprint given to it by God—a unique group of people with unique individual gifts coming together to carry out God's unique mission for them in a particular place during a particular period of time! The Serving Leader is able to continually pull back and interpret this "fingerprint" (big picture) in order to effectively "dive in" and Build on Strength. This is an on-going back-and-forth process, and, as with the other Serving Leader actions, should be based on fervent prayer and the power of the Holy Spirit.

* What would you say is your "sweet spot(s)" in ministry?
* Do you know the "sweet spots" of the people who work/ minster alongside you?
* How could you better align the strengths/gifts of the team(s) you oversee?

Acknowledgements

Elizabeth Wourms

"Therefore, since we are surrounded by such a great cloud of witnesses, let us throw off everything that hinders and the sin that so easily entangles, and let us run with perseverance the race marked out for us. Let us fix our eyes on Jesus, the author and perfecter of our faith, who for the joy set before him endured the cross, scorning its shame, and sat down at the right hand of the throne of God. Consider him who endured such opposition from sinful men, so that you will not grow weary and lose heart" (Hebrews 12:1-3).

Writing this book was a remarkably cathartic experience. Pouring out heart and soul onto these pages demonstrated the formative work God has been and continues to accomplish in me. A Great Cloud of Witnesses surrounds this "Potter's Wheel" experience and these saints participate in God's shaping work. As I write these acknowledgements, I'm overcome with awe and gratitude for the relationships by which God has richly blessed me. Not only did these brothers and sisters in Christ encourage me to run with perseverance, but the fingerprints of their knowledge, wisdom, and experience decorate every page of this text. You know who you are; I couldn't have written this book without you.

I wish I could name everyone whose lives grace these pages, but I must lift up a few in particular who truly are Serving Leaders and have profoundly impacted my life. To my parents, Dan and Stephanie: Dad, I've looked up to you my entire life as an exemplary leader—a man of integrity whose fervent sense of justice and righteousness inspires me and whose commitment to mentor emerging leaders and invest in colleagues invites me to a similar embodiment; Mom, it's totally cliché, but you have always been the "wind beneath my wings," instilling in me an unshakable belief that I can pursue any dream and attain any goal, and your selfless sacrifices of your own dreams over the years in order to put your family first demonstrated the authenticity of your own leadership—I love you "mora!"; thank you both. To my husband Steve: you've always maintained that a big part of your own ministry is to support me in mine—what an incredible gift that is to me. You support me 100% in all my wild ministry adventures—thank you. The way you lean into God and surrender to His leading makes it possible for me to live my call.

Rev. Dr. Chris Hardy, you have been an incredible friend and partner on this journey of life and ministry. Your heart, soul, mind, and experience weave like threads through the tapestry of this book. Much of the content you and I developed together for our doctoral projects and then for our Equipping Leader training series. I'm deeply grateful for your generous spirit that allowed me to include pieces of our work in this volume. This is your book, too. I trust God to show us opportunities to collaborate in Serving Leader initiatives in the future.

At the tender age of eight, I had a dream to become a writer due to my love of books and reading. It's fun to me to see that childhood vision come to reality. I am the halfway decent writer that I am today due in large part to the mentoring of my dear friend and colleague Rev. Dr. R. Robert Creech. As the mentor of my Doctor of Ministry peer group at United Theological Seminary, Robert invested considerable time and energy in reading and providing feedback on my doctoral thesis, going way beyond the "call of duty." Robert, your red editor's pen has left indelible ink on the fabric of my life as you sharpened and honed my writing skills. I am eternally grateful to you for such a formative gift.

Rev. Dr. G. Edwin Zeiders epitomizes Serving Leadership. I was blessed to work with Ed for a season when he served as the President of United Theological Seminary. I have never met a person who so wondrously embodies BOTH a pastor's heart and shepherding style along with a tenacious, savvy, and strategic visionary leadership. I couldn't wait for staff meeting each week to "sit at your feet" and soak up the devotional thoughts that you always brought which were profound pearls of deepest wisdom. Christ's light shines brightly through you as you love and equip God's people through an authentic investment in them. Thank you.

To the leaders across the country who participated in the Equipping Leader cohorts with Chris Hardy and me, your wisdom and experience ooze from these pages, as well. I cherish the times spent in the training room where we wrestled together with what it means to Upend the Pyramid, to Build on Strength, to Run to Great Purpose. As learner-teachers and teacher-learners, we gave shape to much of this content together. I'm eternally grateful. Most of all, I relish the network of relationships and the deep friendships that God has cultivated in, among, and through all of us together. To our Regional Equippers Network, you are my Equipping/Serving Leader family—what an incredible joy to be on the journey with you. I love you all! A special and intensely heartfelt thank you to Beth Goodrich, a mentor and friend. You were the "domino" that started the cascade in Equipping Ministry for me. None of this would have happened without your insistence that I attend a "Sue Mallory training" early on in my ministry. God used you mightily to instill my call.

Beavercreek Church of the Nazarene provided a rich learning laboratory for me to be "in the trenches" of ministry and to get my feet wet and hands dirty in the work of the church. Thank you to Pastor Keven Wentworth, JC Slone, Scott and Tammy Porter, and all the staff for allowing me to learn, fail, grow, push, stretch, form, and flex my wings. My time at BCN is a "standing stone" on my journey. Glory to God!

To John Stahl-Wert, I will forever remember the day that I received the initial email from you inviting me to consider joining you in this writing project. Thank you for listening to God's voice, for being willing to take a risk with me, for inviting me into the realm of Serving Leaders. This invitation is not unlike inviting me through the front door, past the living room, and into the kitchen. The kitchen is where true community forms and vulnerable sharing takes place. I don't take this for granted and I am humbly and profoundly grateful.

"Thank you" doesn't cut it, but thank you.

John Stahl-Wert

It is a distinct joy for me to see this work come to life. From the ministry and calling of my friend, Elizabeth Wourms, from the biblical and theological reflections I've given over the years to Serving Leadership, from the churches and businesses I've coached and offered training, and from the book my friend Ken Jennings and I wrote on The Serving Leader, this book has emerged, filled with applicable tools for the people of God to use in strengthening the witness of the church in the world. I thank God for all of this.

To Elizabeth Wourms, bravo on a terrific body of writing and work! Your steadfastness in driving this project forward, taking the lead, and being diligent to the task was so inspirational to me. And beyond your deeply grounded reflections and excellent writing, there is the serving leader, daughter of God, and great friend that you are. It has been a joy to work with you.

Special thanks to Bob Shull and Neil Brem for putting extraordinary time and love into this manuscript. You strengthened and improved our work immeasurably! Thanks also to Lisa Slayton, Rick Wellock, Jim Van Eerden, Ken Smith, Dan Hupp, Sarah Spicuzza, and Adina Cucicov for speaking into our learning about Serving Leadership over this year and for assisting in the production and publication of this book. And thanks ten thousand times over to Milonica Stahl-Wert, my beloved life companion, for your fierce belief in and advocacy for the things we've been called to serve together. My love to

About the Authors

Dr. ELIZABETH WOURMS is the Executive  Pastor at the Dayton Vineyard Church, Dayton, Ohio (www.daytonvineyard.com). She served as Senior Leadership Team member for Transformational Leadership Connection, a leader consortium and resource center for leadership development and equipping ministry. Her life mission is *to invest in leaders and equip them for personal, organizational, and community transformation.* Elizabeth understands leadership to be *the facilitation of another's becoming,* and she finds joy in serving as a catalyst to release potential in other leaders and the people with whom they serve. Elizabeth played a key role in launching Kingdom Connections of Greater Dayton, a faith-based non-profit organization committed to community transformation. She was formerly the Involvement Pastor at Beavercreek Church of the Nazarene, Beavercreek, Ohio, and Director of the Pohly Center for Supervision and Leadership Formation at United Theological Seminary in Dayton, Ohio. Elizabeth also serves as adjunct faculty for the Seminary. Elizabeth is a REAL Ambassador for Group Publishing, serving as a consultant, writer, and trainer for Group's Church Volunteer Central Association. Elizabeth holds bachelor degrees from Kansas State University and the University of Cincinnati, and a master of divinity and a doctorate of ministry from United Theological Seminary. She is wife to Steve and mother to sons Jacob and Joe; and daughter Lisa McGarry and son-in-law Jon. Contact Elizabeth at ewourms@att.net.

 **Dr. JOHN STAHL-WERT** is President and CEO of the Pittsburgh Leadership Foundation and Serving Leaders, a position he has held since 2000. Serving Leaders equips, connects and mobilizes business and community leaders to "transform the culture of Pittsburgh by building the character of its leaders." In 1994, John became national Training Director for Leadership Foundations of America, and prior to that post he served God's kingdom as a pastor, a missionary and an artist. He earned a bachelor degree from Eastern Mennonite University, a master's degree in Theological Studies from Associated Mennonite Biblical Seminary and a doctorate of ministry from Eastern Baptist Seminary. A gifted storyteller, John is co-author of the international bestseller, *The Serving Leader* (in eight languages), co-author of *Ten Thousand Horses* (in four languages), and author of *With: A True Story*. John is Senior Fellow for the Center for Executive Leadership and a monthly columnist for *Business Management Review*, both based in Beijing. He serves as Adjunct Faculty for Bakke Graduate University (Hong Kong) as well as for Geneva College's Masters of Science in Organizational Leadership. John is a member of the National Speakers Association. He is husband to Milonica and father to Emma and Clara. Contact John at stahlwert@ servingleaders.com.

For resources on how to become a serving leader, and more information on training and workshops, please visit us at: **www.theshipcompany.com**